UNDERSTANDING STRESS IN DOCTORS' FAMILIES

To our children Tony and Natalie

Understanding Stress in Doctors' Families

USHA R. ROUT
Manchester Metropolitan University, Manchester

JAYA K. ROUT
Kearsley Medical Centre, Kearsley, Bolton

LONDON AND NEW YORK

First published 2000 by Ashgate Publishing

Reissued 2018 by Routledge
2 Park Square, Milton Park, Abingdon, Oxon OX14 4RN
711 Third Avenue, New York, NY 10017, USA

Routledge is an imprint of the Taylor & Francis Group, an informa business

Copyright © Usha R. Rout and Jaya K. Rout 2000

All rights reserved. No part of this book may be reprinted or reproduced or utilised in any form or by any electronic, mechanical, or other means, now known or hereafter invented, including photocopying and recording, or in any information storage or retrieval system, without permission in writing from the publishers.

Notice:
Product or corporate names may be trademarks or registered trademarks, and are used only for identification and explanation without intent to infringe.

Publisher's Note
The publisher has gone to great lengths to ensure the quality of this reprint but points out that some imperfections in the original copies may be apparent.

Disclaimer
The publisher has made every effort to trace copyright holders and welcomes correspondence from those they have been unable to contact.

A Library of Congress record exists under LC control number: 00132819

ISBN 13: 978-1-138-72744-1 (hbk)
ISBN 13: 978-1-138-72735-9 (pbk)
ISBN 13: 978-1-315-19088-4 (ebk)

Contents

List of Tables and Figure vi
Foreword vii
Preface viii
Acknowledgements x
About the Authors xi

1   Stress and the Medical Profession   1

2   Stress in General Practitioners   25

3   Stress in Women Doctors   51

4   Overseas Doctors and Families   74

5   Doctors' Spouses and Children   94

6   Managing Stress   112

References   140

List of Tables and Figure

Table 2.1	Job stressors identified by GPs: Factor analysis of stressors	39
Figure 2.1	The six broad sources of stress identified in our study showing how the outcome is a direct response of a GP's perception of the sources of stress and his skill in coping with them	40
Table 2.2	Type A Questionnaire	47

Foreword

The National Health Service is undergoing enormous changes, which has led to many health care workers experiencing pressures beyond their control and ability to cope. The doctors and nurses are particularly under strain from 'change fatigue' in a Service which is constantly changing and demanding more and different procedures and accountability. The role of the doctor, whether the GP or hospital doctor, has altered beyond all recognition from just a decade ago, and continues to face new demands and challenges. The long working hours, the changing perceptions of the doctor by the general public and the spillover of work into family life is taking its toll on this group of dedicated practitioners (as it is on their nursing colleagues as well). The doctors, their colleagues and support staff are not the only ones to be affected by these pressures, the families of doctors and nurses also have to take the brunt of this stress.

This book is a welcome addition to the literature in highlighting the issues confronting not only the doctors themselves but also the families of doctors, their day to day experiences and how they cope or don't cope. Understanding this process and the issues involved can only help us as a community to ensure that we support and help this most valuable human asset, as well as appreciating what this job can do to significant others as well. Congratulations to the authors for their sightful and important book.

Professor Cary L. Cooper, BUPA Professor of Organizational Psychology and Health at the University of Manchester Institute of Science & Technology

Preface

This book is the product of our work on doctors and their families. The interview data that forms its substance includes more than 120 doctors, their spouses and their children that we have interviewed over 12 years of our research. We have organised this book in five chapters beginning with medical students, junior doctors and consultants' stress. Chapter two focuses on specific problems experienced by general practitioners. The content of the third chapter outlines the experiences of women doctors and their family lives. In chapter four overseas doctors, their spouses and their children talk about their experiences which are characterised by cultural diversities. Doctors from overseas often feel themselves subject to prejudice and discrimination and their wives feel lonely and isolated. The advantages and disadvantages of experiencing a range of cultural influences are explored for the children. Chapter five focuses on the experiences of non-doctor spouses and children's point of view. The non-doctor spouses include housewives, working wives of doctors and husbands of lady doctors. The final chapter reviews issues raised by the doctors, their spouses and their children. Suggestions are given to problems to different groups and outlines some individual and organisational stress management strategies.

We have changed the names and identifying information of the doctors and their family members in the case studies and quotations so that anonymity is protected. If the names of individuals in this book bear any similarity it is purely accidental. The views presented in this book are ours.

This book is aimed at medical students, hospital doctors and their spouses, general practitioners and their spouses, other health care professionals and students in medicine, social sciences and allied health professions. Also this book can be of value to the counsellors helping doctors and their families suffering from emotional problems.

Although we have attempted to present an objective view in this book it is inevitable that the views of the authors are likely to emerge as we are a husband and wife team, a general practitioner and a University lecturer in Psychology, whose life very much revolves around medicine and the study of stress in it. We hope that this book will stimulate further debate on doctors and their families in what we believe is an area of growing importance in medicine.

Note: The term 'he' is often used only for convenience.

Acknowledgements

Our special thanks to Carolyn Kagan and John Cavil for their invaluable comments and suggestions on the first book draft; Prodeepta Das and Iain McLean for proof reading the script; Saima, Rahila and Sarah (Usha's PhD students) for their help in literature search, and Marilyn for her secretarial help. It has only been possible to write this book due to the cooperation of all those general practitioners, hospital consultants, junior doctors, their spouses and their children who gave their valuable time to share their experiences. Finally, we wish to thank our children Tony and Natalie for their patience while writing this book.

Thanks to Kluwer Academic Publishers for giving permission to use the material Figure 2.1 and Table 2.1 from *Stress and General Practitioners* (1993).

About the Authors

Usha R. Rout is Senior Lecturer in the Department of Psychology and Speech Pathology at the Manchester Metropolitan University in Manchester. She received her PhD from UMIST and is an Associate Fellow of the British Psychological Society. Dr Rout has authored two books and published several research articles on the subjects of stress and the medical profession, stress and health of health care professionals, and women and work. She is a Fellow of the Royal Society of Arts, Royal Society of Health and Royal Society of Medicine.

Dr Jaya K. Rout is a general practitioner at Kearsley Medical Centre in Bolton. He is co-author of *Stress and General Practitioners* (Kluwer Academic Publishers). He has published several scholarly papers on stress in health care professionals and depression. He lectures to doctors and other health care professionals and conducts stress management workshops.

1 Stress and the Medical Profession

The first part of this chapter provides a brief review of literature on the physical health, mental health, alcohol consumption, cigarette smoking, drug abuse and suicide among doctors. The second part of this chapter covers literatures on stress among hospital doctors and qualitative data from the interview with junior doctors and consultants.

Stress and physical illness

There are several physical diseases which are caused by stress or aggravated by persistent stress. Some of the common stress disorders are described in this chapter. Psychosomatic disorders are the diseases which are believed to have psychological factors as their causative agents. However, psychological factors are linked to specific psychosomatic diseases such as ulcers, rheumatoid arthritis, asthma and headaches (Friedman and Booth-Kewley, 1987). Stomach ulcer is often caused by increased acid secretion into the stomach called hyperacidity. Hyperacidity is thought to be partly associated with psychosocial factors, such as hostility, anxiety and rage (Weiss, 1984).

Circulatory diseases which include heart attacks and strokes are amongst the principal causes of death in 1992 in England among males and females (Social Trends, 1994). It has been proven that hypertension and heart disease are accepted as having a link to stress. Cardiovascular disease is the most prominent killer in industrial nations. Coronary Heart Disease (CHD) accounted for 27% of all deaths in the UK in 1990 and strokes accounted for 12%

of all deaths. In 1990, 83% of deaths due to CHD were in people over the age of 65 and for stroke the corresponding figure was 92%. In the UK, CHD accounts for 30% of all male deaths and the corresponding figure for females was 23%. The incidence of stroke increases with increase of age for both men and women (HMSO, 1994).

Research in the area of occupational stress and health has attempted to determine which working conditions are associated with CHD risk, for example, the psychological demands of the job, autonomy on the job and job satisfaction, work overload and low levels of control over one's job, seem to be particularly important in affecting stress levels in the job. A case control study by Alfredson et al (1985) revealed that increased risk of myocardial infarction was associated with job and occupations characterised by hectic work and low levels of control over work pace and degree of variety. In the two-dimensional job model, Karasek (1979) demonstrated that high job demand and low decisional control are associated with increased CHD. His job demand - control model has been tested in several populations and predicted CHD and mortality in two studies of male Swedish workers and in numerous studies in the USA (Karasek, et al 1987; Theorell and Karasek, 1996).

Retrospective case control studies have found a significant association between CHD and long working hours under stress (Miles et al 1954; Russek, 1959) and professional difficulties in the past (Blohmke et al 1969; Bruhn et al 1968). Prospective studies demonstrated the relationship between financial problems or non-specific stress and incidence of angina (Floderus, 1974; Medalie, 1973; Wilhelmsen, 1980). Other studies have shown a significant correlation between workload or tension at work and the incidence of myocardial infarction (MI) (Shekelle et al 1983; Theorell, 1977).

Physical illness among doctors

It might be expected that doctors would suffer more illness than the general population, because of paramount work pressure, very little free time, long working hours, irregular meals, disturbed nights, interrupted evenings and weekends and close contact with death and diseases. However, the physical health of doctors appear to be better than their mental health (BMA, 1992, 1993).

During the 1950s doctors were almost twice as likely as the general population to develop a myocardial infarction (Morris, Heady and Barley, 1952). During the 1970s it was found that deaths from heart disease have been declining in British doctors, and that doctors under 54 years were less likely to die of ischaemic heart disease and myocardial degeneration than the general population (Doll and Peto, 1976).

In the USA death from heart disease has been more common amongst doctors than in a control population (Dublin and Spiegelman, 1947; Dickinson and Martin, 1956). For example, Dublin and Spiegelman (1948) showed that the rate of cardiovascular disorders was 1.8 higher than that of general population. There may be, however, differences between those in different branches of the profession. For example, Russek and Sohan (1960) found that anaesthesiologists and general practitioners reported two to three times the levels of CHD of dermatologists. It was also revealed that general practitioners were twice as likely as other British doctors to develop myocardial infarction (Morris et al 1952).

By analysing the statistical data published by the Registrar General in Occupational Mortality it can be verified whether doctors have an overall life expectancy different from that of general population. These use the Standard Mortality Ratio (SMR) as a measure of risk. SMR is the ratio of observed deaths in a population divided by those expected from the national death rates, standardised for age and sex, and multiplied by 100. The figures (Registrar General, 1978) showed that overall, doctors have a standard mortality ratio of 81 (that is in 1978 they were 19% better off than the general population). American studies also reached similar conclusions (Dickinson and Martin, 1956; William et al 1971). Similar results in expected deaths was reported among medical students and young doctors (Everson and Fraumeni, 1975). In the years 1938-1942 doctors in general had almost the same longevity and mortality as the general population (Dublin and Spiegelman, 1948, 1949). In the years 1969-1973 during which the medical population reached almost 345,000 with doctors' deaths averaging about 3,800 annually (Goodman, 1975). When doctors were compared with the US white population of the same age and sex, doctors' deaths were lower representing 74.7% of expected deaths in the control group of males and 84.1% in white females.

To sum up: studies of physical illness in doctors are scarce; however, mortality studies are usually retrospective which permit assumptions generally.

Stress and mental illness

A commonly held belief is that workers who are prone to psychiatric illness tend to have background of low socio-economic status and low educational achievement. Thus, they tend to work in low skill occupations (Kasl, 1973; Schuckit and Gunderson, 1973). This assumption has been challenged by others (e.g. Cooper, 1980). The reaction to stress differs in white collar workers and blue collar workers in that the former reflects the pressure of work in mental illness whereas the latter do so in physical symptoms and illness (Cooper, 1980).

Mental illness among doctors

Doctors usually dislike admitting their own illness. They don't realise that they are as susceptible to illness as their patients. The true prevalence of mental illness among doctors is less known than their physical illness and the available studies seem to inflate the incidence. Most include inpatients with severe mental illness. In addition not only do doctors treat themselves but also seek out a doctor colleague who is a specialist in that particular condition. Therefore, the results may not be most accurate in the following studies.

In the past (1969-1972) there have been some major studies of doctors under treatment for mental illness as reviewed by Murray (1978). The percentage diagnosed as having affected psychosis ranged from 21 to 40% and those with schizophrenia ranged from 2 to 12%. Drug addiction and alcoholism were very common (Murray, 1978).

Most of these studies reviewed by Murray (1978) are retrospective. One prospective study by Vaillant et al (1972) consisted of observation of 47 medical students who graduated, and matching controls, over a period of 30 years. During that period 17% were hospitalised for psychiatric illness, 34% underwent psychotherapy (control was 19%), 36% used drugs, whilst only 22% control did so. The numbers here are small but the trend is fairly consistent, and it accords with other studies. It was reported that doctors were more likely to have poor marriages; to abuse alcohol; and to use sleeping pills, amphetamines, or tranquillisers in comparison with other professionals (Vaillant et al 1970; 1972). The reason given by addicted doctors were overwork, fatigue and physical illness. In a British review of psychiatric illness in doctors, Rucinski and Lybulska (1985) concluded that the most common diagnoses remained alcoholism, drug addiction and depression. Between a quarter and a third of preregistration doctors are reported to be suffering from clinical depression (Firth-Cozens, 1987).

Another study by Jones (1977) on 89 male and 11 female doctor inpatients, showed that affective disorder and drug abuse were higher than in the general population. Psychoses, especially schizophrenia, were in general slightly lower except for manic depressive illness which was almost double when compared with general hospital discharges. Neuroses and personality disorders were higher. Alcohol and drug addiction were three times than that of the hospital population.

Murray (1977) studied the admissions to, and discharges from all Scottish hospitals of male doctors aged 25 years and over. He compared them with the figures for all social class 1 non-doctor males. The overall mean of first annual admission rate was 449 per 100,000 for male doctors and 203 per 100,000 for the non-medical males of social class 1. It was revealed that the rates were higher among doctors for all diagnostic categories except personality and behaviour disorders, but the differences between doctors and non-doctors were not significant for schizophrenia, other psychoses and neuroses. The study reported that the rates for drug dependence, alcoholism, and depression were significantly more common among the doctors than non-doctors, particularly in middle age. Fifty-eight percent of all doctors hospitalised between the ages of 45 years and 54 years were alcoholics.

The prevalence of mental illness in medical students is shown in several studies. It was reported that 25% of students seek psychiatric help before graduation from medical school (Bojar, 1971). Salmons (1983) examined medical school records for the past 25 years at a British University and found that 2.4% had been reported as developing a psychiatric disorder and 1% required hospitalization. She noted that total psychiatric morbidity was likely to be considerably higher since students are often treated for their problems which might not have been entered into their medical records. It was estimated that between 15 and 25% of medical students met the criteria for a psychiatric diagnosis (Lloyd and Gartrell, 1984). The difficulty with this study, as with many other questionnaire surveys, is that response rates were low (39% of students replied), and only one medical school was investigated.

In a longitudinal study, Firth (1986) used the 12 item version of the General Health Questionnaire (GHQ-12), a measure of perceived strain used in a number of occupational studies, at three British provincial universities for fourth year medical students. It was found that mean strain levels among medical students (11.66 on the GHQ-12) were considerably higher than comparable groups within the normal population (8.67). Thirty percent of students fell into psychiatric caseness category compared with 9.1% in a comparable sample of young employed men and women. This study makes its findings particularly important because of its high return rate (i.e. 78.5%). However, it is worth remembering that the non-respondents tended to be more depressed than those who responded (Vernon et al 1984).

Nevertheless, it may be possible that all these findings are illustrations of high strain levels in students as a whole rather than in medical students alone. Therefore, let us look at a comparative study between different types of students. Bjorksten et al (1983) compared medical students with other health-oriented student groups (dentists, pharmacists, nurses and allied professions) at their university. The finding was that medical students revealed a wide range of problems which were significantly more intense than the other groups.

It may be possible that medical students get less sleep, less time for recreation and have a higher number of working hours which make them a particularly vulnerable group. This notion is supported by a study by Friedman, Kornfield and Bigger (1973). The finding was that when interns were deprived of sleep they felt significantly more fatigue, dejection, sadness and perceived themselves to develop several psycho-physiological abnormalities. The psychological problems reported were depression, difficulty in thinking, irritability, referentiality, depersonalization and recent memory deficit.

Added to the problem of sleep deprivation and other intrinsic stressors, it is possible that the family history of medical students might be contributing to their psycho-physiological abnormalities. Fifty four interns were studied and it was found that 30% of them suffered from depression; four of them had suicidal ideation, three had suicidal plan and six had marital difficulties with their depression (Valko and Clayton, 1975). It was also found that the depressed interns had a positive family history of depression and a family history of suicidal attempts. Waring (1974) claimed that the family history of mental illness, life experience and the personality before entering medical school are of greater importance in the formation of psychopathology than the occupational hazards of medical practice. It was found that unstable childhood and adolescent adjustments were critical variables in physicians with poor marriages, drug or alcohol abuse, or psychiatric difficulties (Vaillant et al 1972). Interns whose personalities are well integrated and who have strong self-esteem may fare better than those with unresolved conflicts (Werner et al 1979). Nadelson and Notman (1979) note that "the factors affecting vulnerability, distress and symptom formation are complex: the nature, the number and magnitude of the stresses and individual personality factors and capacities must all be considered".

Suicide

Government statistics show explicitly, higher suicide rates for doctors compared with other professionals such as lawyers, school teachers, the clergy and of course the general public (Bennet, 1982).

The 1970-1972 Decennial Supplement (HMSO, 1975) revealed that the major diseases from which doctors are more likely to die than the general population are suicide (SMR - 335), cirrhosis (SMR - 311), and accidents (SMR - 180). In Britain, doctors are nearly 3.5 times more likely to commit suicide than the general population (HMSO, 1978).

Suicide among doctors

Doctors are among the ten highest risk occupation for suicide; they have a suicide risk of 72% higher than the general population (McKevitt et al 1995). In America, Blachly et al (1968) reviewed all the Obituary notices in the Journal of the American Medical Association between 1965 and 1967. Two hundred and forty nine suicides were reported giving an annual suicide risk for doctors of 33 per 100,000, close to the average for all white males in the USA. Steppacher and Mausner (1974) studied 530 deaths (489 male and 41 female physicians) by suicide in a five and half year period. They noted that suicide rates for male physicians was 1.15 times that of the total male population and for female physicians it was three times.

Rose and Rosow (1973) have revealed the inaccuracy of the above studies by reviewing all death certificates of males in California from 1959 to 1961 and showed that physicians, and health care workers as a group, are twice as suicide prone as the general population. The doctors who tend to kill themselves were relatively young (i.e. half the suicides in male doctors studied by Rose and Rosow occurred between 35 and 54 years of age).

Sakinofsky (1980) looked at data (Office of Population Censuses and Surveys, England and Wales) on the civil states of the 55 male doctors (age 25-64) who committed suicide during 1970-1972. It was found that unmarried and divorced doctors tend to be more suicidal (age group 35-54). Twice as many doctors among the suicides have remained unmarried than among other living doctors, and there were also a disproportionate number of increase in divorces. However, it would not be wise to conclude anything from this data due to the small sample size. But we may speculate that there is some form of threat.

The American Psychiatric Association and the American Medical Association co-sponsored a study in 1986 to find out suicidal death of physicians. Those physicians who died a suicidal death were compared with a control group who died from natural causes. It was found that 219 physicians were reported to have killed themselves between 1982 and 1984. Of the original 219, 142 interviews were obtained from survivors of suicide. Also the family members of two control groups were interviewed: family members of those dying from natural causes (68) and those dying of ambiguous circumstances (33). Of the 142 suicidal cases, 129 were male and 39 were female. Sixty-nine percent of the entire group was married or living as married at the time of suicide whereas only five of the female physicians were married. Sargent (1986) argued that the results 'implicated biological heredity and premorbid personality as causative factors of suicide. The stresses particular to life in medicine are seen as aggravating factors which may differently affect women'. This study showed that presuicidal physicians show some mental health problems which include prior suicidal threats, chronic illness at the time of death, a history of psychiatric treatment, self-prescribing drugs, prior suicide attempts, prior psychiatric hospitalization, violence to spouse, sexual problems in marriage, acknowledge drug abuse, smoking, blaming self for illness and financial loss in the two years before death (Scheiber, 1987).

Suicide amongst physicians may be due to their wrong choice of career. It was found that students who were inclined towards artistic and literary careers before entering medicine were more vulnerable to the signs and symptoms of strain and expressed significantly more suicidal ideation than those students who were inclined to pursue a scientific career (Schwartz et al 1978).

Nevertheless, it is evident from the above studies that doctors are prone to suicide. Clearly, the recording of suicide is minimal (Rose and Rosow, 1973), for one cannot be certain how many suicides go unrecognised and reported as accidental. It can be suggested that a bigger longitudinal study based on psychological testing of the current medical students may provide information on the specific traits of those who later commit suicide.

Alcohol consumption

The proportion of men and women consuming alcohol is highest amongst those in the employers and managers socio-economic group. In the UK the recommended maximum sensible amounts are 21 units per week for men and 14 units per week for women. (The limits have been increased recently to 28 units for men and 21 units for women). The percentage of men exceeding these guidelines is much higher than that for women (Social Trends, 1994). The cost of alcohol-associated illness in the UK was estimated at £1,687 million in 1986 (Marmot and Brunner, 1991) and the overall social cost is around £2.5 billion today (Health Update, 1993).

It was estimated by the Health Education Authority (1987) that over eight million working days are lost each year due to alcohol consumption. In a number of studies different occupational groups showed varied alcohol drinking problems. For example, Hingley and Cooper (1986) in their sample of nurses found that 8% of nurse managers consumed alcohol on a daily basis, compared to 4.8% of the female population. In another study of oil rig workers, Sutherland and Cooper (1987) reported that 61% often consumed alcohol during onshore leave as a method for stress relief.

In a study in the USA, Margolis et al (1974) interviewed 1,500 employees in a variety of occupations, and discovered a positive relationship between escapist drinking and a number of specific stressors. Those experiencing high job stress drank more than those in occupations where there was low job stress. It is considered by some authors that the presence of high levels of stress at work can lead some individuals to resort to heavy drinking as a coping technique (Hurrell and Kroes, 1975). However, it is not clear why some people under stress become alcoholics and others control their alcohol intake. It is suggested that the influence of genetic factors plays a significant part in severe alcoholism among men. But it is important to make distinction between severe alcoholism and problems with drinking. Sutherland and Cooper (1990) suggest that a genetic component could be the basis of certain characteristics, which could play a significant part in alcohol consumption and tolerance to alcohol.

Alcoholism among doctors

It was found in a study in Scotland that the first admission rate for alcohol dependence was 2.7 times higher among doctors than among controls (social class 1) (Murray, 1978). The average weekly consumption of alcohol by male medical students was similar to that of the men of matched-age in the general population. On the other hand, for female medical students the alcohol consumption was higher than that of women of matched-age. A recent nationwide survey of 1,278 medical students found that in a typical week 17% of the respondents exceeded the recommended limits for sensible drinking (Ghodse and Howse, 1994). In addition, the study found that 10% of the respondents were current smokers and 10% were ex-smokers, 37% of the respondents used other drugs.

Several studies showed that medical professionals are especially susceptible to cirrhosis, suicide, poisonings, accidents, and alcohol addiction (Allibone et al 1981; Bennet, 1982; Murray, 1978; Lloyd, 1982). This may be detrimental to the individual doctor's health. However, doctors do not like to discuss the problems with colleagues and peers like to ignore the symptoms of stress in their colleagues (Rawnsley, 1985, Symons and Persaud, 1995). The problems found here may be the tip of the iceberg. It was estimated that there may be as many as 3,000 practising general practitioners in the UK who are alcoholics, while many others may show other signs of stress (Allibone et al 1981). It was revealed that 13,000 - 22,000 doctors in the USA were alcohol dependent at some stage in their career (Bissel and Jones, 1976).

The literature on impaired physicians showed that in 1980, 1,608 impaired physicians were in contact with the State Medical Society Programmes. Drug and alcohol abuse problems appear more common in male doctors (The Impaired Physicians, 1978). Gomberg (1979), on a national level, reported that there were approximately 4 to 5 male alcoholics for every female alcoholic.

However, alcohol consumption appears to be associated with relatively low risk of CHD in a number of studies (Marmot, 1984). In two prospective studies (The US Nurses Health Study and, the Health Professionals Follow up Study), alcohol consumption was associated with a significant reduction in risk of CHD (Stamfer et al 1988; Rimm et al 1991). Nevertheless, other longitudinal studies show higher total mortality in heavy drinkers, but predominantly due to causes other than CHD (Boffetta and Garfinkel, 1990). Alcohol drinking can adversely affect cardiovascular disease through its effect in increasing blood pressure at intakes above 4 units of alcohol a day. This could partly account for the increased risk of stroke (HMSO, 1994). Therefore, the risk of alcohol consumption outweighs the benefit.

Cigarette smoking

In the UK, large number of deaths are due to smoking related diseases, such as lung cancer, respiratory disease or heart disease, which could be prevented. High proportion of unskilled and manual workers smoke heavily (Social Trends, 1994). The percentage of men who smoked cigarettes fell by 8% between 1982 and 1992 while the percentage of women who smoked cigarettes fell by 5%, at a slower pace, from 32 to 27% (HMSO, 1994). However, in spite of the knowledge that smoking cigarette causes death and illness, people continue to smoke in large numbers and now 28% of adults are regular smokers (Health Trends, 1994).

A study of more than 10,000 UK myocardial infarction (MI) survivors has shown that non-fatal MI rates are five times greater among smokers than non-smokers (Parish et al 1995). The risks were greatest in the 30-49 age group, three times more common in smokers than non-smokers in the 50-59 age group, and twice as great at ages 60-79. Not only is smoking related to heart disease incidence, but also it is associated with neuroticism and anxiety (McCrae et al 1978). Hennigan and Wortham (1975) expressed the view that people who are not smokers and are in good physical condition, are all able to maintain low heart rate during the normal stress of the working day, whereas stress is more likely to increase the heart rate of people with less physical fitness.

Cigarette smoking among doctors

Between the years 1972 and 1980 the proportion of smokers in all groups fell, especially among professionals (Social Trends, 1983). Doctors were among one of the first groups of individuals who gave up smoking once its harmful effects were known (Registrar General, 1978). It was found by Golding and Cornish (1987) that fewer medical students were smokers or illicit drug users than non-medical students. Doll and Peto (1976) demonstrated the beneficial effects achieved by doctors due to decreased smoking. The SMR for doctors from lung cancer was 35% of that expected for the general population (HMSO, 1978). Smoking can be seen as a form of palliative coping which provides temporary relief (Lazarus, 1981). Hence, giving up smoking may promote health but residual tension may remain which in turn influences the behaviours in a damaging way such as excessive alcohol drinking and self-prescribing of drugs (Lloyd, 1982; Bennet, 1982; Murray, 1978, 1983). Smoking was one of the most commonly identified ways of coping with stress among nurses (Hawkins et al 1983).

Drug addiction among doctors

Many investigators emphasized that drug abuse is an occupational hazard for doctors. Norwood East (1949) found that of the 383 known addicts in the UK 82 were doctors. It has been shown by the General Medical Council (GMC) between September 1980 and August 1981, that out of 51 doctors investigated, 19 were classified as drug addicts or alcoholics (reported by Baily, 1985). The medical profession in the UK has expressed its serious concern about drug dependency and alcoholism amongst doctors (Irvine, 1982; HMSO, 1975).

In the USA, one study reports a 20-year follow-up of 45 physicians who were originally described as 'psychologically unsound'. On follow-up, they found that a large number continuously engaged in self-medicating with drugs or regularly abused alcohol (Vaillant et al 1970, 1972). The reasons given by addicted physicians were overwork, fatigue and physical illness. Doctors inclined to prescribe for themselves which often leads to concommitant drug addiction (Murray, 1977; Bissell and Jones, 1976). Usually such physicians are reluctant to present for treatment and sometimes commit suicide (Murray, 1977).

In addition to the series of mentally ill doctors previously reviewed, in all of which drug addiction was common. Drug addiction was claimed to be present in 17% of doctors as reported by a'Brook et al (1976). According to the US Commissioner of Narcotics (Anslinger, 1957) the general population showed a rate of 1:3000 drug addiction. A psychiatry professor at the University of Arizona (in the Medical World News, 1984) reported that more than 4000 physicians in the USA were known addicts.

There have also been specific old studies of drug-dependent doctors (Pescor, 1942; Wall, 1958; Modlin and Montes, 1964). Putnam and Ellingwood (1966) followed up 68 addicted doctors discharged from Lexington Hospital; the major drugs of addiction were morphine, mepiridine and barbiturates. Green et al (1976) reported on a study of 46 Virginia physicians covering the period 1947-1974. The drugs used in order of frequency were 'hard' narcotics, ataraxics and stimulants, used alone or in combination with narcotics. Most frequently addicted doctors were general practitioners and internists.

It thus appears that there is evidence of drug abuse due to the stresses of the doctors' occupations. However, Green et al (1976) viewed that a combination of predisposing personality disorder and the easy availability of drugs were the main reasons of drug abuse among physicians.

Sources of stress in medical students

James Knight (1981) points out that it is important to understand the motivation of a person, who applies to study medicine, which influences their acceptance of a place and the chances of future success. He identified a broad pattern of motivational factors which grouped into three categories: (i) motives stemming from inner needs; (ii) motives stemming from vocational appeal; and (iii) motives stemming from conceived purposes.

(i) There are many motives stemming from inner needs. For example, relationships with parents may play an important role in choosing medicine as a career. The needs to control one's fear of death as well as the need to help others may be important factors. In addition, the inner need for financial security cannot be overlooked.

(ii) Motives stemming from vocational appeal could include the image of the doctor, medicine as a challenging vocation, and work freedom. The image of a doctor in society possesses lasting appeal and a medical career offers a great many challenges. In medicine, doctors have a lot of freedom to choose their own method of working.

(iii) Motives stemming from conceived purposes could include providing nurturing relationship to others. The students who are attracted to medicine may have been propelled by their close contact with physical or psychological suffering and a desire to be devoted to removing suffering.

The professional socialisation of medical students takes place in an environment which has been described as rigid, authoritarian and dehumanising (Knight, 1981). Medical students struggle to strike a healthy balance between their personal and professional lives (Gaensbauer and Mizner, 1980). Researchers have found some stressors (e.g. academic demands, no time for social and ecreational activities) for medical students in different schools and different cultures (e.g. Coburn and Joviasas, 1975: Canada; Firth, 1986: England, Wolf, 1994: USA) Medical education can change the lifestyle of medical students in their first year. For example, Wolf and Kissling (1984) revealed that physical activity, sleep, general health, leisure and recreational activities were decreased among first year medical students. Research evidence suggest that during medical education attitudes, values, mood and personality change.

For example, Wolf et al (1989) have shown that graduating medical students perceived that they became more cynical over the course of their medical education.

In a study of Norwegian students, stress was a good predictor of mental health and consistent with USA schools findings (Bramness et al 1991). Stewart et al (1995) surveyed medical students in Hong Kong and found that the students were concerned about the medical school curriculum and environment. Loss of opportunity to maintain social and recreational sources of gratification correlated with anxiety. Active coping styles correlated positively with distress. In the USA, Wolf (1994) reviewed the literature on stress, coping and health of students during medical education. The conclusions drawn were used as a basis for recommendations to improve medical education. The author emphasised the incorporation of the principles of health promotion and disease prevention throughout medical education in order to prevent and minimise burnout.

Although numerous cross sectional studies found high level of stress among doctors, few have used longitudinal data to investigate possible precursors that might allow early prevention or intervention. One study by Firth-Cozens (1997) is worth noting. She followed up a group of general practitioners from their fourth year undergraduate education to find out the importance of early symptoms of stress and self-criticism in predicting stress levels after 10 years. She found that self criticism was a strong predictor of stress symptoms over a long period. She suggests that by recognising vulnerable students (for example - when tutors see signs of self blame in clinical discussion) it is possible to reduce stress symptoms in future doctors. The personality traits which moderate the stress effects are: high level of commitment; internal locus of control and great sense of challenge. Kobasa (1979) named this particular style of personality as 'hardiness'. It is suggested that when selection of medical or nursing students is undertaken the personality hardiness factor should be considered (Fain and Schreier, 1989).

In another longitudinal study, conducted six times from first to the last year, it has been found that at least 12% of the class showed depressive symptoms at any assessment during the first 3 years and

25% during the end of the second year (Clark and Zeldow, 1988). Other researchers revealed that self esteem and positive mood decreased while negative mood increased during first year medical education (Wolf, 1994). However, more longitudinal studies need to be conducted to follow medical students beyond graduation so that assessment on attitudes and personalities could be performed.

Sources of stress in junior doctors

King et al (1992), in London, sent 320 questionnaires to hospital doctors to study past and current emotional distress, sources of stress, effects on work and home life, type of help sought and perceived outcome of that help. They found that the doctors are subject to high levels of personal distress and the doctors experiencing emotional distress have difficulty in disclosing this to anyone outside their immediate family and friends. They did not seek professional help from counsellors or support from their colleagues. The commonest problems were difficulties with partners, withdrawing from people and personal disorganisation. The effect of past distress was greater for preregistration and junior doctors than for consultants. (King et al 1992). The authors explained that stress in hospital doctors do not decrease with seniority but the pressure differs, the consultants have more control over their management of workload and with experience they might have learned to adapt to the stress. The ethos in the medical world is to deny health problems especially mental ones. The reported stress in this study is striking.

Bulstrode (1991) suggests that junior doctors are being squeezed on the one side by the management who has no money for a locum and on the other side by consultants who demanded of them the highest standards of medical practice without considering the cost of the well- being of junior doctors. He commented that the amount of time spent on committees and management by many consultants seems to be reducing the value to the health service by not spending as much time as they should for patient care.

A study examined the occurrence of major personal events in residents' lives and changes in behaviour or attitude among house officers across training years (Taylor et al 1987). The findings suggested that there were certain patterns of events and behavioural and attitudinal changes which might be exacerbating the stress of residency (Butterfield, 1988). Williams et al (1997) surveyed 171 senior house officers and found an inverse relation between psychological distress and confidence in performing tasks in accident and emergency departments. The study concluded that there is a need to monitor and build confidence in senior house officers. However, further details could be found from Butterfield's (1988) excellent review of the literature on stress of residency.

We carried out research on junior doctors during 1993. In-depth interviews were conducted with 23 junior doctors in different parts of England. The main aim was to investigate major sources of stress among junior doctors. The interviews lasted from 30 to 90 minutes. The interviews were aimed at exploring personal and professional aspects of medicine especially stress related to the job and possible overflow of stress into family life, and also coping strategies. In the latter case respondents were asked to think of and describe a recent incident or situation which they found particularly stressful, and to describe the coping strategies they employed (critical incident technique-Dewe, 1991).The main sources of stress for junior doctors were sleep deprivation, work overload, long working hours, night call, lack of time for self, family and friends and responsibility for patients. These stressors are also found by other researchers (Firth, 1987).

One of the doctors from our interview sample expressed his dissatisfaction regarding his heavy workload and lack of time for his family.

> I do not have time for my wife and my two year old daughter. Every week I plan something with them, but most weeks I do not make this happen due to the pressure of work. Sometimes I am so tired I do not like to go out with them. I used to play piano and play tennis but now with so little time it is difficult to keep up with these. I gave up most of the things now.
>
> (SHO, age 30)

Likewise:

> I am continuously racing against time. Too much to do in too little time. So much demand on my time......I can't work faster than this. My personal relationships are not maintained properly. My partner is very unhappy about me not spending enough time with him. I have no energy and time for him. I haven't seen my close friends for months.
>
> (Woman SHO, age 29)

Another doctor said how he saves his time by not socialising:

> I used to go out with my friends regularly. Due to pressure of work I socialise very little now. I feel I am cut off from the rest of the world. I lost lot of good friends now. I feel isolated.
>
> (SHO, age 29)

Other themes running through the interviews were anxiety over reporting death to relatives, loss of sleep and examining patients of opposite sex.

> It was very stressful for me when I had to report the death of a child to his parents for the first time. I think I was not trained properly for this and I felt I was not quite prepared for this. I was very anxious and stressed out.
>
> (SHO, age 27)

Lack of sleep was one of the major complaints by many of the junior Doctors:

> I am tired after continuous on call in a weekend. I get irritable because of the sleep loss. Some weekends you are up all night ... drinking coffee and seeing patients. At the end of the duty you are collapsing.
>
> (HO, age 24)

> Lack of sleep and long hours makes me dull and lethargic. I do not feel like doing anything I feel like catching up with my sleep all the time.
>
> (SHO, age 28)

Examining patients of the opposite sex, was one of the stressors for young doctors.

> I don't feel comfortable to examine female patients when nurse is not there.
>
> (SHO, age 25)

When asked about how did they cope with stress, a commonly used strategy expressed by them was drinking.

> I like to have a drink with my friends.
>
> (SHO, age 26)

The detailed analysis of this study can be found elsewhere (Rout, 2000).

Sources of stress in consultants

Consultant posts are top of the hospital professional ladder. Becoming a consultant in the British NHS is a long, highly demanding and competitive process. These doctors have to pass a rigorous exam to become fellows of their Royal Colleges. Traditionally, consultants have enjoyed higher status than community doctors and general practitioners. The consultants see patients referred by the general practitioners. The number of consultant posts is limited in relation to the number of senior doctors appointed in the hospital.

Within medicine, certain specialities are considered as being more prestigious than others. For example surgeons who specialise in brain or heart appear to have higher status than those who are specialising in psychiatry and geriatrics (Baggot, 1994). Many of the sources of stress in doctors are common to different specialities, but there may be specific pressure related to particular medical speciality and different stages of medical career (BMA, 1992). For example, research in the USA has reported that some medical specialities (i.e. anaesthetics and general family practice) are inherently more stressful than others, resulting in greater 'physician impairment' (Talbot et al 1987). A comparative study of consultants and general practitioners showed that consultants had greater occupational stress and had greater job satisfaction overall than general practitioners. Females had less occupational stress and greater job satisfaction overall than males (Swanson et al 1996).

A British Medical Association (BMA) questionnaire survey of 1423 consultants found that two thirds of the respondents felt their job satisfaction would decrease as a direct result of the NHS changes (BMA News Review, June 1991). On the other hand, 91% did not regret taking up a career in medicine. This suggests that the changes in the working environment were causing increased stress and dissatisfaction, rather than their clinical responsibility. Caplan (1994) surveyed 81 hospital consultants, 322 general practitioners and 121 senior hospital managers. General practitioners were more likely to be depressed than managers and there was no significant difference between hospital consultants and general practitioners. General practitioners were significantly more likely to show suicidal thinking than were consultants but not managers. However, the level of stress, anxiety and depression in consultants, general practitioners and managers in the NHS seem to be high.

In a national questionnaire-based survey, in the UK, Ramirez et al (1995) reported that prevalence of psychiatric disorder in consultant oncologists was 28% and they had equivalent levels of emotional exhaustion and low personal accomplishment compared to those found in American doctors and nurses (Maslach and Jackson, 1986). The sources of stress identified in this study - for example, being overloaded, work effects on home life, dealing with patients suffering and being involved with treatment toxicity and errors - appear to be similar to other doctors (Rout and Rout, 1993, 1994; Firth Cozen, 1987) and cancer health professionals of all disciplines (Cull, 1991). Also organisational responsibilities/conflicts were found to be one of the most important stressors for these consultants. The authors explained that these may be due to the ongoing changes in the NHS in the UK. Another finding was that the doctors who felt insufficiently trained in communication and management skills had significantly higher levels of stress than those who felt sufficiently trained.

A workload survey showed that average hours of work of consultants have been increased in excess of their contractual commitment and there has been a dramatic increase in non clinical work (Beecham, 1999). Another workload survey showed that there had been a shift in workload from junior doctor to consultants (Beecham, 1999). The Central Consultants and Specialist Committee's chairman said, "quality of patient care is bound to be affected when we are cramming more and more patients through our clinics" (Beecham, 1999).

We interviewed 30 consultants in the North West of England (Rout and Rout, 1998). Qualitative analysis of the data revealed that time pressure and work overload are two important stressors for the consultants. Other stressors identified were NHS changes, no family and social life, lack of resources, conflict with management, unpredictable demands, pressure to keep up-to-date with new developments, and increased expectations by patients. There are some differences between different specialities. For example, consultants in obstetrics and gynaecology had major pressure from the increase in complaints and litigation, whereas for surgeons major operations going wrong was the major source of stress. All the consultants were satisfied with the clinical aspects of their job rather than administration.

The stressors and coping strategies concerning consultants are discussed below very briefly. The full study can be found elsewhere (Rout and Rout, 1999). All the consultants said their stress was due to time pressure: lack of time in the outpatient clinic, long lists, and less time spent at home were the main issues.

> We are under pressure to fast track patients and treat them within a short period. I think this is an exercise to show that large number of patients are being treated in the hospital. Surely this is a number game. It does not tell you how many patients are readmitted due to complications. Obviously the figures get inflated. We work hard under severe time pressure.
>
> (Male, cardiologist, age 49)

> There is far too much demand and I have to kind of work during the week on a regular basis and also during weekends. I don't have that much time. The junior staff are not that experienced to delegate that much, so you got to keep going yourself all the time. Again the core arrangements have changed to their favour so much that you kind of hardly speak for yourself. And when I have major cases the junior doctors are not in a position to help and there are complaints about waiting times.
>
> (Male, gynaecologist, age 56)

Government's publication of Patients' Charter has placed 'patients first' in the National Health Service. The charter, in many ways, has increased patients expectations and encouraged unrealistic demands. According to the charter the patients have to be seen within half an hour of arrival in the outpatient department. This can never be guaranteed under the current circumstances.

> Some patients demand that their operation must be carried out by a consultant only, not by any junior doctor. The junior doctors need to do operations, of course under supervision of the consultant, to gain practical experience. Otherwise how are they going to treat their patients when they become consultants.
>
> (Male, gynaecologist, age 46)

Interviewees were asked what they do during their off duty hours. These consultants adapted variety of hobbies.

Dr Carlson was a consultant physician in an urban hospital in the north of England. He grew vegetables in his greenhouse, and was an expert at growing tomatoes. Dr Kaplan played violin in an orchestra and wrote for medical newsletters. Dr John was an amateur photographer for many years and won many prizes in several competitions. Dr Symonds, a surgeon, painted pictures using water colours, which made his house like an art gallery. Other doctors played football, tennis, badminton and squash in their local clubs. The most popular game was golf for our doctor sample. Not only men played golf, we found some golfers in our women sample as well. Women doctors in our sample took part in community work in addition to their medical commitment.

Conclusions

We have presented a brief literature review on hospital doctors and some qualitative results of our study. The major stressors for the consultants were: time pressure due to long lists in the outpatients, lack of time at home and unrealistic expectations by the patients. The important stressors for junior doctors include: lack of socialisation due to lack of time, inadequate sleep, continuous on-call, very little time for the family. The purpose of the next chapter is to discuss stress among general practitioners and their families. Although some of the stressors are common to both genders, we shall concentrate on female doctors and their families in the third chapter.

2 Stress in General Practitioners

The aim of this chapter is to discuss occupational stress among general practitioners and its effects on the individual. Firstly, literature on stress in general practitioners will be addressed and secondly our qualitative and quantitative studies will be discussed. The final section will include type A behaviour, coping and social support as these influence the experiences of occupational stress.

There have been a number of published works on sources of stress and the health among general practitioners (Porter et al 1985; Makin, Rout and Cooper, 1988; Rout and Rout, 1993, 1994; Chambers, 1992, Chambers and Belcher, 1993). Constant time pressures, heavy workload, problems of practice administration, home/work conflict and emergencies are among some of the stressors for general practitioners (Porter et al 1985; Howie et al 1989; Rout and Rout, 1993, 1994; Rout, Cooper and Rout, 1996).

In addition to this, doctors are increasingly exposed to malpractice suits which seems to have some relationship to job dissatisfaction (Richardson and Burke, 1993; Charles, Wilbert and Franke, 1985; Mawardi, 1979). Many doctors express feeling depressed and frustrated, report less satisfaction with their practice and consider early retirement (Richardson and Burke, 1991). A study of the health and lifestyle of general practitioners and teachers showed that self medication was common among general practitioners (Chambers, 1992). It was found from a study that a high proportion of doctors smoked and drank alcohol excessively (Allibone, Oakes and Shannon, 1981). This may be detrimental to the individual doctor's health.

Recent enforced contractual changes for general practitioners in the UK caused widespread dissatisfaction, due to both accelerated change and a lack of consultation with ordinary members of the profession (Bain, 1991). The National Health Service and Community Care Act in 1990 have created a new role for general practitioners as purchasers of care for their patients. General practitioners are now expected to work in a multidisciplinary team. They are having to be more accountable for the way in which they spend taxpayers' money. Medicine has become more business like and general practitioners may have to face stress and strain in balancing the demands of these new roles (Van Sell et al 1981). It is believed by some authors that the profession no longer has the same respect and prestige as in the past and that the potential for satisfaction may have been reduced (Sutherland and Cooper, 1992).

Karasek's (1979) job strain model predicts that job strain results from the combination of low job decision latitudes (constraint in decision making or less control over the task) and heavy job demands. He classifies general practice occupation as a high demand and high decision latitude profession which means high demands of the job will not be encountered as stressful while there is also autonomy in decision making. When the freedom is withdrawn the high demands of the job may become unbearable. Following the introduction of the new contract in 1990 the general practitioners have suffered greater restriction to their autonomy and they reported that they no longer felt in control of events that affected their working practice (Rout and Rout, 1994). It was found from the British Medical Association survey that 88% of doctors felt that they faced greater stress in their working lives than five years ago. Doctors have not adapted to the changes imposed on their working environment (BMA News Review, 1996).

Recently Appleton et al (1998) assessed the levels of psychological symptoms, job satisfaction, and subjective ill health in general practitioners in Leeds, UK. They found that 52% of the doctors showed high levels of psychological symptoms and 60% felt that their physical health had been affected by their work. The doctors expressed their least satisfaction with their hours of work, recognition for their work and rates of pay. In an international comparative study it was revealed that British general practitioners experienced less job satisfaction, poorer mental health and significantly greater pressure at work than did their Canadian counterparts (Rout and Rout, 1997). Canadian doctors perhaps have more freedom to choose their own method of working but the British general practitioners, however, are still encountering policy changes and experiencing external pressure exerted on them.

Levita's (1995) study found that lack of control, ambiguity and change were amongst the sources of stress in general practitioners. Most importantly he noted that the general practitioners did not mention any positive outcomes of stress i.e. stress was not regarded by the general practitioners as a source of challenge, interest or creativity. It is important to see the positive side of stress as it is significant in individual's ability to cope (Kobasa and Puccetti, 1983).

Bates (1982), with a sample of Australian general practitioners, found that 'physical overwork' was the main stress that was caused through medical practice. In a study of general practitioners job satisfaction and quality of prescribing, Melville (1980) found low job satisfaction to be associated with higher levels of prescribing of certain drugs with potential adverse side-effects. She suggested that job dissatisfaction appeared to be correlated with frustration and gave two reasons for this. According to her, the personality characteristics of some general practitioners might not match the requirement of general practitioner work. Secondly, certain aspects of the general practitioner's task could lead to dissatisfaction. Mechanic (1972) found that time factors were major sources of dissatisfaction for physicians in the primary care setting. Grol et al (1985) found that negative feelings about work (i.e. frustration, time pressure, tension) correlated with a high rate of prescribing and a reluctance to provide an explanation to patients. Positive feelings about work (i.e. satisfaction, feeling at ease) were correlated with a more open approach to patients and more attention to the psycho-social aspects of the complaints.

Another study revealed that general practitioners are more likely to be depressed and show suicidal thinking than senior health service managers and hospital consultants (Caplan, 1994). Other authors have found that general practitioners reported depression and anxiety frequently as problem areas (Chambers and Belcher, 1993).

After the introduction of the new contract, Sutherland and Cooper (1992) found a fall in job satisfaction and an increase in anxiety and depression in 1990 when compared to 1987. Even before the introduction of the 1990 contract, it was found that the work of general practitioners makes them particularly prone to anxiety (Rout, 1989).

It is important to investigate the workload of general practitioners as work overload is one of the main stressors for doctors. A study by Porter et al (1985) gives in-depth information about the time allocation for different activities of general practitioners. The aim of their study was to analyse the relationship between workload, stress, job performance and quality of care in general practice. Eighteen doctors were studied over 3 days in three group practices in Edinburgh. They used interview, diary and questionnaire methodologies to find out workload, work-flow, self-perceived pressure and stress, and stressor-mediating or intervening factors (personality, biography, attitudes/orientation, and social support). The average stress score was 4.7 and there was a wide range of values of 'stress' per doctor (3 doctors had an average stress score of 0 and one doctor had an average score of 10, maximum = 14). The practice with the slowest consultation rate recorded the lowest proportion of pressure scores and the practice with the fastest consultation rate recorded the highest proportion of pressure scores. The findings show that there is a high degree of individual variability in experiencing stress and the rate of consultation is proportional to the pressure score. Therefore general practitioners might consider consulting patients at a slower rate. The authors suggest that it is important to understand the behavioural changes that might occur when the general practitioner is challenged by stress and the subsequent consequences on patient care.

Morrell et al (1986) found that doctors could not cope with a booking session of five minutes interval but there was a wide variation (i.e. range of 0.7 to 29 minutes per consultation). However, shorter consultation times are associated with increased antibiotic prescribing and longer consultation times are associated with increased identification of psycho-social problems. There was no evidence of increased stress as a function of shorter and more frequent consultation but the doctors were unhappy about the shortage of time.

Our study

To date, one of the largest UK studies investigating occupational stress among general practitioners was carried out by the authors in the 1980s (Rout, 1989; Cooper; Rout and Faragher, 1989; Rout and Rout, 1993) and more studies in the 1990s (Rout, 1996; Rout and Rout, 1997). In-depth interviews were carried out with general practitioners, their spouses and their children. The detailed analysis of the spouses and children's interviews will be reported later. The interviews were aimed at exploring stress in general practice, especially stress related to the job and possible overflow of stress into their family life and highlighting the coping strategies used.

Data from the interview was wholly qualitative. Responses to questions about sources of stress and coping strategies were analysed to identify recurrent themes concerning sources of stress at work and at home. The stressors and coping strategies concerning male general practitioners will be discussed here.

When the general practitioners were asked to what extent they found their job stressful, 100% indicated that they experienced moderate to high stress at work. When asked, 'what exactly do you find stressful in your job?', all general practitioners considered paperwork to be a high pressure activity. Other stressors included:

- time pressure
- being on-call/night calls
- work overload
- interruptions
- increased demands by patients/unrealistically high expectations of the general practitioners role by others
- lack of communication
- lack of support from spouse
- aggressive patients

- financial stress
- bureaucracy
- lack of resources

Time pressure

All the general practitioners in this sample felt very busy most of the time and some of them commented: 'work never ends'. Typical comments were:

> When I was single handed I was really very busy and I thought by having a partner I would get a bit of time off. Even with an additional partner the surgeries are getting longer and longer and I am finding it difficult to catch up with paperwork. It is strange that I am now spending less time at home than I did before.

> If I had time I would enjoy my work. The pressure of speed of work with no respite for 11 hours a day produces unbelievable frustrations. Little inclination on 'the day' to attend postgrad meetings, read journals etc. which all add greatly to job satisfaction. Things are so bad, every day I think about giving up. You've got me at a bad time – it's 8.00pm and I've been working since 8.30am - no stop for lunch.

> The single most important cause of stress in my life is the way my work affects my family life. My children aged 2½ and 5 are already aware that there are times when I cannot be available and often cannot be approached even though I am at home.

On-call/night call

General practitioners have a contractual obligation to provide 24 hours cover for their patients. Some general practitioners use deputising services or co-op if available in their areas but other general practitioners have to provide cover for their patients themselves. They have to remain on-call during day and night. Interrupted sleep at night to answer the telephone, giving advice to patients, or visiting patients, is not only stressful but also detrimental to their health. Disrupted sleep may also affect their judgement the following day.

Typical comments were:

> There is no deputising service available in my area. I have to do my own night calls. Recently the number of night calls have increased significantly and as a result my sleep is being disrupted and my family gets disturbed as well. I feel really exhausted and irritable the next day.

> Night calls produce follow-up stress because of the tiredness factor and not being quite up-to-the mark by the end of the next day. Much worse as one gets older, having coped in ones early days in practice.

> There is stress when on-call even when not working because one cannot settle fully to any task as it may be interrupted. One cannot plan one's time.

> Weekends on-call are a 'nightmare' especially if they are very busy. A light weekend can be almost as bad, waiting for something to interfere with whatever you might be trying to do.

Work overload

Work overload can be seen as being quantitative or qualitative. Quantitative work overload refers to too much to do and qualitative work overload refers to too difficult work to do. The following illustrations describe quantitative work overload where the general practitioners are pressurised by over-whelming paperwork and administration.

> The ever increasing waiting list for outpatient appointment and admissions with the increased workload, frustration and patient dissatisfaction that this brings.

> The present system whereby the general practitioners have to prescribe for patients attending hospital. This again increases workload especially as time is required to explain the reason why patients have to make several journeys to obtain their drugs.

The ever increasing proliferation of paperwork relating to general practitioner dispensing. A lot of this appears to be entirely unnecessary.

Interruptions

Comments made by general practitioners during the interviews suggest that interruptions of any kind are considered as very stressful. It is not only irritating to the doctor but also distressing to the patient when the general practitioner is in the middle of consultation. For example, as a general practitioner stated:

> My surgery staff have been given strict instructions not to interrupt during a consultation unless there is something very urgent. Invariably one of the receptionists would ring through during surgery consultation, often to ask if the call should be considered as urgent.

Increased demands by patients

From the interview sample it was learnt that the general practitioners felt pressurised in meeting the increasing demands made by patients, as illustrated by the following quotations from some of our interviews.

> I have been in general practice for 21 years and enjoyed it thoroughly. But after so many years I am leaving the NHS and going into alternative medicine simply because the patients' demands have increased to such an extent that I find it difficult to cope with.
>
> I am becoming increasingly intolerant of people who 'abuse' the free medical service to which they are entitled. I feel most stress when I have to visit someone for medico-legal reasons to be on the safe side. Within my short working experience people are turning to their doctor far more frequently now for less and less important reasons.
>
> Anti professional attitude by many patients who attack doctors under the going of Consumer interest.

Now that there is the Patient's Charter and the demands from patients. The patients forcing the doctor for certain medications and begging for sick notes. .... Really non-medical things shouldn't be dealt by doctors and are cropping up more these days, because of the new regulations.

A lot of things which I find difficult here which is people with unemployment. They would ask a number of items on their prescription, which I feel is bit demanding.

Whilst they are going away, 'while I'm here can you put me some paracetamols; can you give me a cough bottle; can you give another cream for my skin.' I have a shopping list and I don't pay for prescription because I am unemployed so why not take it off doctor. These things I dislike.

Lack of communication

It was found from the interview sample that general practitioners are poor communicators. The senior partner/s assume that the junior partner/s would perform the job the way he/she was conducted it in the past. There are also problems of communication among general practitioners and practice staff.

This is illustrated by the following quotations:

> Whenever the practice manager tries to fix a practice meeting the senior partner is always reluctant to participate, but whenever he does he wants to impose his ideas on others. We don't get a chance to express our views and there remains a big gap in our understanding.

> Old partner 74 years plus. He works part-time but shares 50% surgery earnings. He has full control of administration. Hinders patient management on modern times - hinders proper work by staff, fiddling with it. Discourages smears - investigation of patients - discourages maintaining records - frequently on holidays, I have had no holidays for 3 years. Partner does no on-call commitment. I am on-call everyday. In brief I have considerable degree of stress as I am unable to provide the care I would like to the patients. Despite my long hours and full responsibility for the patients on the list of 3,800 I am not compensated by the remuneration I receive.

Lack of support

Lack of emotional support from spouses was one of the major complaints. As a young general practitioner married for one year admitted:

> I get no emotional support at home. I feel that my blood gets sucked at work and I would need sympathetic attitude from my spouse to recover but this does not happen.

Another example:

> At the moment there are some problems at home due to lack of time. As more time is spent in the practice it creates misunderstanding. But basically we have a sound marriage and good understanding and support, though naturally it wears thin at times!

Aggressive patients

Some of the general practitioners in the interview sample felt threatened by aggressive patients as following extracts explain:

> Aggressive patients, who in the first place have something in mind to demand and when they don't get their own way they start turning nasty. Even they can turn it into a situation of assault, which I have had before really. I got hit by a drug addict. I had to call the police. I had to wait until the police came and I got a few things smashed up in the surgery and things thrown about in reception.

> In the evenings anybody could attack. Anybody from the main road can enter and you don't know the patient and who is coming with some motive.

> Dealing with aggressive/demanding patients and lower socio-economic group family.

> The increasing aggressive attitude of some patients.

Financial stress

General practitioners are being expected to provide the best quality service to patients but without any additional resources provided to them. Therefore general practitioners are facing financial strain.

> Having the financial stress -having to employ a lady doctor to act as assistant. I am the only practice in this area without a lady partner and my patients need access to a lady doctor, just as the patients of other practices have access to a lady doctor.

Bureaucracy

General practitioners feel that they have lost their independence because the Government and the Health Authorities restrict their activities.

> Nowadays FHSA pressure, compulsory computers in the surgery etc - Undoubtedly Government is inspired in order to destroy NHS general practice as it is today.

> Interference by the FHSA. This has now become too prevalent and act as a disciplinary body.

> Government interference in changing of so called self-employed general practice.

Lack of resources

It appears that lack of resources was one of the top stressors for general practitioners.

> Difficulty in getting patients into hospital, when necessary. It is all too easy to say – 'Sorry we have no beds'.

Coping

When asked about how they coped with stress and tension which they experienced, a commonly used strategy expressed by them was having an alcoholic drink in the evening after returning from the surgery. Other coping strategies included exercise, gardening and listening to music. As one general practitioner put it:

> As soon as I arrive at home I treat myself with a good glass of gin and tonic without which I can't relax.

It is worth noting a classic case of alcoholism.

Dr Fox was spending a lot of time in a local pub, even during the lunch time. When he was conducting surgeries one could smell alcohol on his breath. All his partners in his surgery knew this but nobody liked to tell about this. This may be due to denial of the problem in a doctor colleague, embarrassment, modesty in approaching the partner or simple avoidance. This went on for quite a long period. We found out after a few months that Dr Fox died due to cirrhosis of the liver.

The younger doctors may have different values towards these problems as a young doctor reported a case of alcoholism of his senior partner to the Local Medical Committee.

> Once I saw my senior partner consulting the patients after drinking whisky. I didn't like this. I wanted to help him. I reported this to the Local Medical Committee. They helped him but reported to the General Medical Council (GMC). He was reprimanded by the GMC. He decided to pack in and take earlier retirement. I felt very guilty about it. But I thought I did the right thing, otherwise patients health would have been in danger.

Majority of doctors reported negative stress manifestations, psychological, physical and behavioural. The range of symptoms that general practitioners suffered is revealed by the following quotes:

Very busy and stressful time at present with changes in the practice, working often to 1 am with paperwork. Therefore very tired and feel faint/giddy at times, but sleep very soundly, though not always refreshed after 6 hours sleep or less.

It would probably be helpful for you to know that I was separated from my wife and children in December, following which I was off work with 'General Debility', and at that time I was denying that there was anything wrong other than tiredness or "burn out". I worked from March to May with great difficulty. At the end of May I felt unable to cope at all, because there was nobody at home to relate to. I was admitted to a psychiatric unit and diagnosed as having "Bipolar depression". It was suggested that I consider resignation from the health service on medical grounds - but have decided to return to work on Monday 5th October. At the age of 40 I am loathe to stop working at a job that I originally enjoyed. It's very difficult to assess whether stress within the marriage produced more stress at work or vice versa. What is certain is that the breakdown has lowered my powers of concentration and memory recall to a point whereby the next few months will be difficult. Having once been very self-confident, my confidence and self-esteem have taken a downhill slide that will be difficult to regain.

I have now been a general practitioner for about 10 years and enjoyed the work very much and felt quite happy about being a general practitioner until my retirement. However, at first I became severely depressed and experienced all the worst aspects of life as a general practitioner. - long hours, no family life, no holidays and no adequate pay. All this lead to a prolonged period of depression and ill health, from which I have now fully recovered, but it leaves me with the feeling that I need not have experienced these things if adequate support and guidance had been available to me early on in my career.

Ophthalmic herpes zoster while partner was on holiday - continued working, reached exhaustion, had two and a half weeks sick leave.

I feel that people's expectations have risen to a level that I find it difficult to cope with. Recently one of my patients was given a prescription for a morphine injection during the morning. One of her relations requested a visit at 10pm because they hadn't collected the injection from the chemist and the patient was in pain. I had no morphine with me but I offered pethidine instead. The relative insisted on morphine which at that time was not available even through emergency chemists. As a result of her insistence the patient did not have any pain killers and suffered from pain. Few days later I received a letter from the Family Health Services Authority (FHSA) that a complaint has been lodged against me because of my unsympathetic attitude, and the hearing will take place next month. I know that I've done nothing wrong but I have been feeling very uneasy since I received the notification. I realise that I am losing concentration during surgery consultations. I have no patience to listen to patients' symptoms. When I return home at the end of the day I get irritable with everybody at home. I do not like to play with the children. I can't sleep well. I have nightmares thinking of the outcome of the hearing. I had given up drinking and smoking six years ago but started again. I find it difficult to discuss my problems with anyone.

Quantitative study

Study 1

A national sample of general practitioners was studied (Rout and Rout, 1993) to identify sources of job stress associated with high levels of job dissatisfaction and mental ill-health. We carried out in-depth interviews with 49 general practitioners during 1987. A questionnaire was constructed for distribution and then piloted on a sample of over 100 general practitioners in the North West of England (Makin, Rout and Cooper, 1988). This questionnaire, along with other valid measures, were sent to a random sample of 4,000 general practitioners throughout England, achieving a response rate of 48.2%. The final sample for statistical analysis was 1,817, of which 1,474 were male (81.1%) and 343 were female (18.9%).

The stressor items were analysed to identify common stressor themes or patterns. These items grouped statistically into six factors or themes, such as, demands of the job and patients' expectations, interruption, practice administration, work/home interface and social life, dealing with death and dying, and medical responsibilities for friends and relatives (table 2.1). The model of stress in general practitioners illustrates the sources of occupational stress and subsequent stress outcomes, based on our findings (see figure 2.1).

Table 2.1 Job stressors identified by GPs: Factor analysis of stressors

Factor 1: Demands of the job and patients expectations (62.8% of variance)
    Fear of assault during night visits
    Visiting in extremely adverse weather conditions
    Adverse publicity by media
    Increased demands by patients and relatives for second opinion from hospital
    specialists
    No appreciation of your work by patients
    Worrying about patients' complaints
    Finding a locum
    Twenty-four hour responsibility for patients' lives
    Taking several samples in a short time
    Unrealistically high expectations by others of your role

Factor 2: Interruptions (10.6% of variance)
    Coping with phone calls during night and early morning
    Night calls
    Interruption of family life by telephone
    Emergency calls during surgery hours
    Home visits
    Dealing with problem patients
    Remaining alert when on call

Factor 3: Practice administration and routine medical (8.6% of variance)
    Hospital referrals and paperwork
    Conducting surgery
    Practice administration
    Arranging admission
    Working environment (surgery set-up)
    Time pressure

Factor 4: Home-work, interface and social life (7.7% of variance)
    Demands of your job on family life
    Dividing time between spouse and patients
    Demands of your job on social life
    Lack of emotional support at home, especially from spouse

Factor 5: Dealing with death and dying (5.5% of variance)
    Daily contact with dying and chronically ill patients
    Dealing with terminally ill and their relatives

Factor 6: Medical responsibility for friends and relatives (4.4% of variance)
    Dealing with friends as patients
    Dealing with relatives as patients

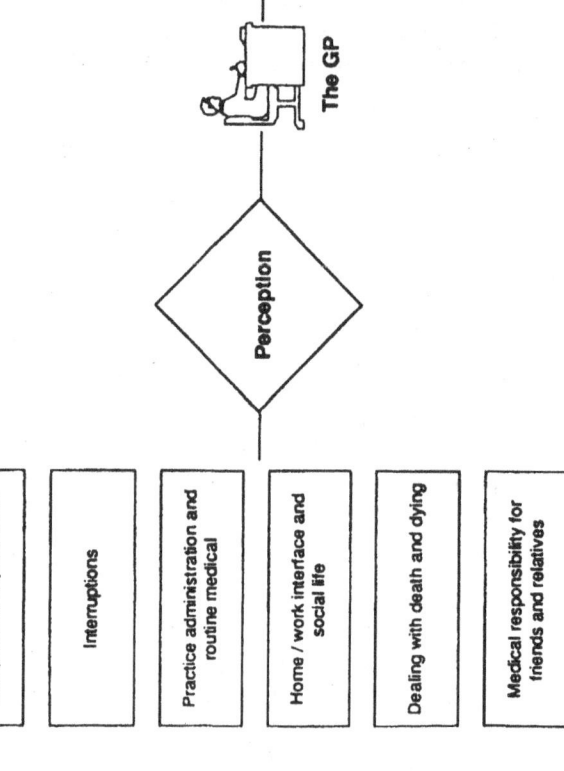

Figure 2.1 The six broad sources of stress identified in our study show perception of the sources of stress and his skill in coping with t

It was found that female general practitioners were significantly more satisfied with their job than their male counterparts. Satisfaction was the greatest with intrinsic features of the job, that is the amount of freedom, responsibility and variety in the job. The lowest job satisfaction levels were the extrinsic factors, such as hours of work and rate of pay. Male general practitioners had significantly higher levels of anxiety than the normative comparison group. On the other hand, female general practitioners had significantly lower scores on the anxiety, depression and somatic anxiety scales. Both male and female general practitioners reached higher mean scores in Type A behaviour scale than the senior male and female managers (Rout and Rout, 1993). Type A behaviour is discussed in this chapter.

Multivariate analysis was used to identify the predictors of outcome (i.e. mental ill-health and job dissatisfaction). This analysis showed that the stressors associated with the demands of the job, practice administration, interruption and home/work interface were predictive of job dissatisfaction. Predictors of overall mental ill-health included the stressors of practice administration, interruptions, demands of the job and patients expectations and home/work interface. It was concluded that the sources of stress identified as significant predictors of both lack of mental well-being and job dissatisfaction were related to managerial and social skills rather than technical skills. These skills can be developed by training. People management, time management and organisational skills development is likely to help reduce the stress associated with these problem areas at work. Also these skills might help by minimizing the impact of their job on their family life.

Study 2

Our objective was to compare the measures of job satisfaction, mental health and job stress amongst general practitioners, by surveys before the new contract came into effect, and again 3 years later. During December 1993 we distributed 850 questionnaires to a national sample of general practitioners. A total of 414 questionnaires were returned (response rate 48.7%) of which 380

(44.71%) were sufficiently complete for statistical analysis. The sample consisted of 68.9% male and 30.8% female general practitioners. Their ages ranged from 25 to 65. Compared with the 1987 survey it was found that there were slightly more doctors in the middle age group and fewer in the younger and older age groups.

General practitioners showed higher levels of stress in 1993 than in 1987. In addition, general practitioners were less satisfied with their job in 1993 than in 1987. We suggest that this may be due to the great number of changes that have taken place during this intervening period. They have had to work in an uncertain environment throughout years. They have been compelled to fulfil the requirements of the new changes in their job. After the introduction of the new contract, the general practitioners were less satisfied with their job with regard to their hours of work, rate of payment and degree of recognition they receive for their good work. It would appear that most general practitioners feel that they do not receive enough recognition and praise either from patients or colleagues. As mentioned earlier, the high demand nature of general practice is well documented. The accelerated changes in general practice in 1990 was beyond the control of the doctors due to lack of consultation with ordinary members of the profession (Bain, 1991). This has resulted in considerable tension among general practitioners. We suggest that there was a perceived loss of control over their destiny. The findings highlight the importance for general practitioners to have control over their work environment, status in their job and recognition from others for work well done.

Throughout the interviews, and in comments made on the questionnaires, general practitioners expressed unhappiness with the 1990 contractual changes. This was mainly due to the way in which changes were introduced. Furthermore, they are expected to be experts in management skills, but with accelerated change they often felt uncertain about what is going on.

Both male and female general practitioners appeared to be more depressed and had higher levels of somatic anxiety in 1993 than 1987. There has been little work on the effects of this drop in mental health in relation to patient care and its ultimate consequences on general practitioners. Myerson (1990) found that 75% of general practitioners remained at work when they felt ill or exhausted primarily because of locum costs, guilt feelings towards patients and colleagues and work pressure. Doctors are often unwilling to admit their illness and reluctant to accept advice for their psychotic illness (a'Brook, 1990) which is a source of denial. This may be detrimental to patient care.

Personality traits

Why are certain people more vulnerable than others to the stressors they encounter? The individual's personality, coping strategies, life stages, age, sex, ethnic background, previous experience, number and intensity of stressors and degree of social support he/she receives are seen to affect stress vulnerability. It is important to note that situations are not inherently stressful but there are certain personal factors which might make a person more or less vulnerable to stress. Researchers have identified different personality types which appear to be more 'stress prone' than others. We found that general practitioners showed higher type A behaviour scores than managers. To understand this the focus needs to be on doctors personality traits and coping strategies.

Doctors have often been described as intelligent, compulsive, perfectionist, emotionally detached, intolerant of failure and achievement oriented. These traits are acquired by children in dysfunctional families (Ziegler, 1992). Gabbard describes the maladaptive aspects of compulsive traits which include: 'difficulty in relaxing, reluctance to take vacations from work, problems in allocating time to family, an inappropriate and excessive sense of responsibility for things beyond one's control, chronic feelings of 'not being enough', difficulty in setting limits, hypertrophied guilt feelings that interfere with a healthy pursuit of pleasure, and the confusion of selfishness with healthy self-interest'.

Many authors have observed that doctors resist seeking help. They do not ask for help and they think that they should be autonomous, self-sufficient and self-controlled. Actually, they have difficulty in asking for help for themselves when they are under stress. The equating psychiatric symptoms with a sign of weakness has been a common finding. In addition, acknowledging psychiatric symptoms as part of an illness would challenge a doctor's sense of omniscience, omnipotence and invulnerability. As Robinowitz (1983) expresses, 'Physicians may use their knowledge and skills to defend themselves against their own anxiety about strength, both integrity and dangers of illness and health'.

Type A coronary-prone behaviour

In the early 1960s Meyer Friedman and Ray Rosenman (two cardiologists) found that individuals who exhibited certain behavioural traits were significantly more likely to develop coronary heart disease (CHD). The traits were referred to as the 'coronary-prone behaviour pattern' Type A (high risk of CHD), as opposed to the more relaxed 'Type B', who had a low risk of CHD. These cardiologists noted a particular way of behaviour that seemed to be common to their heart patients. For example, type A patients tended to sit at the edge of their chairs as the authors reported that the man doing the reupholstery work commented on the unusual pattern of wear on the front edges of the chairs (Friedman and Rosenman, 1974).

Type A behaviour was found to be the overt behavioural syndrome characterised by 'extremes of competitiveness, striving for achievement, aggressiveness, hyper-alertness, explosiveness of speech, tenseness of facial musculature and feelings of being under pressure of time and under the challenge of responsibility'. It has also been suggested that 'people having this particular behavioural pattern were often so deeply involved and committed to their work that other aspects of their lives were relatively neglected' (Jenkins, 1971). The most significant trait of the type A person is his ceaseless sense of time urgency. Rosenman and Friedman (1974) refer to this pattern as the 'hurry sickness'. On the other hand, type B individuals are characterised by Jenkins et al (1967) as being more relaxed and easy going, rarely becoming impatient, not easily irritated, working steadily without a feeling of being driven by time pressure, and speaking in a slower and more modulated manner. Rosenman et al (1966) express that this dichotomy is not a sharp division as 'the subject with behaviour pattern A simply exhibits to enhanced and sometimes excessive degree and certain traits which are variously present in subject with pattern B but to a lesser degree'.

According to Brief et al (1983) in a work setting, type A individuals:

1. Work long hours constantly under deadlines and conditions of overload;
2. Take work home on evenings and at weekends; they are unable to relax;
3. Often cut holidays short to get back to work or may not even take a holiday;
4. Constantly compete with themselves and others; also drive themselves to meet high, often unrealistic standards;
5. Feel frustrated in the work situation;
6. Are irritable with work efforts of their subordinates;
7. Feel misunderstood by their superiors;

Type A behaviour was a predictor of CHD among men in white-collar occupations. However, the results of some studies have not always found consistent relationships between type A behaviour pattern and CHD. The negative components of type A personality construct are anger, hostility and aggression (Spielberger et al 1985) Research suggests that hostility and aggression are higher in type A people than others (Check and Dyck, 1986). It is worth noting a prospective study of 255 medical students who filled out the Minnesota Multiphasic Personality Inventory (MMPI) (which includes a measure of hostility). The health status of these doctors was assessed (Barefoot et al 1983) after 30 years. It was found that there was a nearly 5 times greater incidence of CHD among the doctors with hostility scores above the median than among those with hostility scores below the median. Also hostility predicted mortality from all causes. The number of deaths was 6.4 times greater among those with the higher hostility scores than among those with the lower hostility scores. The findings are supported by

Shekelle et al (1983) that the mortality rate among males with low hostility (used MMPI) measured 25 years earlier, was 18% compared to a 30% rate among those with high hostility score.

It may be that type A individuals are more prone to perceive stress in an exaggerated fashion (Caplan, 1971). This would appear to be intuitively relevant to studies of stress in general practitioners. It can be suggested that general practitioners with type A personalities may organise their working day differently and may perceive and respond to work overload differently to general practitioners with type B personalities. The general practitioners with type A personalities may take more responsibility, for example, may be actively involved in running the practices, may take more outside work and may not take much responsibility in the family life. They may perceive more workload by working faster but self-record low levels of pressure of part of a denial of that pressure.

It remains to be seen whether the general practitioners were of type A personality before entering into general practice or whether they develop or intensify such personality after entering into the profession. Rosenman (1978) considers that many people do not possess type A characteristics when they enter an occupation but increase time pressures, demands for speed and conscientiousness required by the job can make a relaxed type B into a type A.

A type A questionnaire is given in table 2.2. for your own assessment. This questionnaire, based on work by Bortner will give you an approximate idea of the extent of your type A behaviour. The higher scores being indicative of more type A behaviour. This questionnaire yields scores ranging from 14 to 154 and summing an individual's score gives an overall measure of type A behaviour. The higher scores being indicative of more type A behaviour.

Coping

According to Folkman and Lazarus (1980) there are two functions of coping: problem-focused and emotion-focused. Problem-focused coping involves taking direct action to change a stressful situation

Table 2.2 Type A Questionnaire
YOUR BEHAVIOUR
Could you please circle one number for each of the 14 questions below, which best reflects the way you behave in your everyday life.

For example, if you are always on time for appointments, on question 1 you would circle a number between 7 and 11. If you are usually more casual about appointments you would circle one of the lower numbers between 1 and 5.

Casual about appointments	1 2 3 4 5 6 7 8 9 10 11	Never late
Not competitive	1 2 3 4 5 6 7 8 9 10 11	Very Competitive
Good Listener	1 2 3 4 5 6 7 8 9 10 11	Anticipates what others are going to say (no, attempts to finish for them)
Never feels rushed Even under pressure	1 2 3 4 5 6 7 8 9 10 11	Always rushed
Can wait patiently	1 2 3 4 5 6 7 8 9 10 11	Impatient while waiting
Takes things one at a time	1 2 3 4 5 6 7 8 9 10 11	Tries to do many things at once, thinks about what will do next
Slow deliberate talker	1 2 3 4 5 6 7 8 9 10 11	Emphatic in speech, fast and forceful
Cares about satisfying him/ herself no matter what others may think	1 2 3 4 5 6 7 8 9 10 11	Wants good job recognised by others
Slow doing things	1 2 3 4 5 6 7 8 9 10 11	Fast (eating, walking)
Easy going	1 2 3 4 5 6 7 8 9 10 11	Hard driving (pushing yourself and others)
Expresses feelings	1 2 3 4 5 6 7 8 9 10 11	Hides feelings
Many outside interests	1 2 3 4 5 6 7 8 9 10 11	Few interests outside work/home
Unambitious	1 2 3 4 5 6 7 8 9 10 11	Ambitious
Casual	1 2 3 4 5 6 7 8 9 10 11	Eager to get things done

Scoring: The higher the score, the more you are leading a Type A life style. The score range from 14 to 154, with 84 as an average score.

(for example, by seeking information about what to do or by confronting the individual who is responsible for the particular problem) or to reduce the demands of the situation or increase ones resources to deal with it. Emotion-focused coping attempts to reduce the emotional consequences of the stressful situation, it usually does not change the threatening condition but makes the individual feel better. Individuals rely on both types of coping (Folkman and Lazarus, 1980) to manage stressful situations. One form of coping may be preferred to the other depending on the situation. For example, problem-focused coping could be used when the outcome of an event is appraised as amenable to change, whereas, emotion-focused coping could be used when the outcome of an event is appraised as unchangeable (Folkman and Lazarus, 1980).

Emotion-focused coping is viewed as maladaptive when it prevents direct actions. The example below shows that Dr Patra used emotion-focused coping by avoiding the problems at home and at work.

> Dr Patra had been a general practitioner for 25 years. He was remarried 3 years ago after his first wife died of cerebral haemorrhage. His second marriage was not working well. Also he could not cope with the 1990 General Practitioner contract which had created mounting paperwork. He experienced considerable stress as a result. He maintained his emotional equilibrium by spending most of his time in the pub and socialising with his friends. His drinking behaviour raised concern among his senior partners. He started neglecting his patients and avoided paperwork. He was warned by his colleagues for not keeping up with the paperwork and patient care which was a further source of stress. Dr Patra also recognised that he was avoiding the workload. He did not make any effort to change the problem but relieved his stress temporarily by meeting people in the pub. This helped him in the short term but was ineffective in the long term. He took early retirement, continued drinking heavily and died of liver failure.

However, denial (emotion-focused coping) can be very useful on a short term basis where an individual can do nothing in a threatening situation or when the situation can not be changed, for example, death of a loved one. Research by Billings and Moos

(1981) suggest that usually people tend to use more problem-focused coping than emotion-focused coping. The same authors found that women tend to use more emotion-focused coping strategies than do men. Denial can play a positive role in achieving and maintaining detachment from stress and its sources (Lazarus, 1983) but extensive use of denial is likely to prove counterproductive in coping with stress.

Social support

Researchers have shown that people who lack social support from family, friends and co-workers have more psychological and physical symptoms than those with support. The following example illustrates this.

> Dr Chakraborty who wants to obtain a higher degree and be a consultant got no support from her husband. She worked hard in general practice, prepared for the membership examination and had to look after the house at the same time. The situation gradually went worse and she suffered from stress and depression. She was put on antidepressant therapy by her own general practitioner. Her colleagues were never supportive. She was unable to cope with her work and resigned from her job. She could not discuss domestic problems with anyone at work mainly due to her cultural background and also because she had no close friends. She expressed her unhappiness, during the interview, about not getting any support from her husband. She compared herself with another lady doctor with the same cultural background whose husband had given encouragement and full support at home. As a result, the other lady was able to do a lot of things that she wanted to do.

Gore (1978) found that unemployed people who lacked social support had higher serum cholesterol levels, depression and illness compared to those with supportive relationship. Studies also revealed that a lack of support from spouse or partner was related to poor mental well-being, anxiety and depression among construction site managers (Sutherland and Davidson, 1989). It is well known that social support from the boss or co-workers could benefit individuals in the workplace (LaRocco and Jones, 1978; House, 1981).

Researchers found that the average effect of social support across stressful events is modest and sometimes it has a negative effect on the recipient (Vaux, 1988). It was also found that social support can harm an individual's health (Suls, 1982). Members of the social network with a tendency to intrude may actually make things worse (Lieberman, 1982). Conflict within a relationship may add more to distress than to mitigate (Stephens et al 1987). Other researchers emphasize that even when there is conflict within the relationship high levels of support can be beneficial (Barrera and Baca, 1990; Paget et al 1987).

Conclusions

What is evident from the material reviewed in this chapter is that general practitioners are indeed under pressure of time in the workplace and at home. The main sources of stress for general practitioners were: work overload, being on-call, interruptions, increased demands by patients, lack of communication, lack of support from spouse, financial stress, lack of resources, aggressive patients and bureaucracy. Most of these stressors were found in previous literature (Rout and Rout, 1993, 1994, 1995). Most of the doctors we interviewed reported negative manifestations of stress. This, surely needs more investigation so that these doctors can get professional help. This is described in detail in the final chapter. Type A behaviour, coping and social support are touched upon in this chapter because our studies found that general practitioners exhibit type A behaviour, adapt negative coping strategies to cope with stress and do not like to ask for support. However, these will be discussed in the final chapter.

3 Stress in Women Doctors

The previous chapters have introduced stress among hospital doctors and general practitioners. This chapter will cover stress among women doctors by concentrating on the research literature and qualitative data from the interviews with women doctors.

Women and employment

Nowadays a significant proportion of women participate in the labour market in most western countries. Women accounted for 44% of the UK labour force in 1996 (Labour Market Trends, 1996) and in European labour market women account for 41% of all adults who are in work or looking for work (Plantenga, 1995). These rates are predicted to continue increasing e.g. - three-quarters of women are expected to be working by the year 2001 in the UK (Davidson, 1997). However, today the employment rates are greater among certain groups of mothers: those with employed partners, higher levels of education and higher status occupations (Brannen et al 1994).

The directly employed NHS hospital and community Health Services workforce is predominantly female (75.5%) although the proportion is smaller for medical and dental staff (32.9%) (September 1997) (Pullinger, Dept. of Health, 1998). Now, women medical students average just over 50% of the United Kingdom's annual intake to medical schools (Wilson and Allen, 1994). Despite the increasing number of women entering into medicine they tend to be disproportionately clustered in specialities that are less prestigious and lower paid while mainly absent from higher status and higher paid specialities (Allen, 1988; Maheaux et al 1988). Women are more likely than men to enter a speciality which is not their first choice (Parkhouse and Ellin, 1988) and many more women than men fail to achieve their desired status in general practice (Buchan and Stock, 1990). The proportion of female general practitioners in England and Wales was 18.0% in 1981 and 28.6% in 1993 (Wilson and Allen, 1994) which shows a clear rising trend of female general practitioners entering into general practice.

More recent figure shows that in England, out of 33,227 general practitioners, 30% were female during 1996 (Pullinger, Dept. of Health, 1998). In hospital medical staff, out of 21,039 consultants 16,649 were male and 4,390 female, out of 11,588 registrars 7,525 male and 4,063 female, out of 14,752 Senior House Officers 8,520 male and 6,232 female, and out of 3,447 House Officers 1,662 male and 1,785 female (Pullinger, Dept. of Health, 1998).

Work and family

For most employed adults work and family are the major life roles. When pressures from work and family role are incompatible individuals experience work-family conflict. Evidence suggests that work-family conflict has negative effects on well-being in both work and family (Burke and Greenglass, 1987). There are two main types of work-family conflict: time-based conflict and strain-based conflict (Greenhaus and Parasuraman, 1994). Time-based conflict is experienced when an individual delegates more time to one role which makes it difficult to spend the required time for the other role. Strain-based conflict is experienced when strain caused in one role spills over into the other role.

Women occupy roles that are different to those of men (wife, mother) and roles that are labelled identically (paid worker) but may be structured differently. Much of the literature relevant to multiple role involvement implicitly reflects this distinction. Involvement in both work and family roles has been seen as a source of men's advantage over women with respect to mental health (Gove and Tudor, 1973) and as the source of overload and conflict for women, that is, as detrimental to women's mental health. Long and Porter (1984) argue that underlying this inconsistency concerning the number of roles is the assumption that a particular role that of paid worker is necessary and beneficial for men but is an "added on", hazardous role for women.

Two major hypotheses have been put forward concerning the relation of role involvement to well being. The first hypothesis; called the 'scarcity' hypothesis, was first put forth by Goode (1960) and extended by Coser (1974), and others. According to the scarcity hypothesis, people do not have enough energy to fulfil their role obligations, thus role strain is normal and compromises are required. Therefore the more roles one accumulates, the greater the probability of exhausting ones supply of time and energy and of confronting conflicting obligations, leading to role strain and psychological distress. This hypothesis was developed to account for men's behaviour in formal workplace organisations. When applied to women, the assumption is that family roles demand total allegiance and energy. Accordingly when women assume the role of paid employee, a role that exposes them to the demands of the organisation, the net affect is hypothesised to be debilitating. The scarcity hypothesis assumes that women have limited resources with which to meet the demands of the workplace.

In contrast to this view, the 'expansion' hypothesis (Marks, 1977) emphasises the benefits rather than the costs of multiple role involvement. They argue that rewards such as self esteem, recognition, prestige and financial reward more than offset the costs of adding on roles. Benefits include status, privileges, increased self esteem, and the ability to trade off undesirable components of roles. According to this view, involvement in several roles is likely to mean having a variety of stimulation, gratification, and social validation. This view is supported by the work of researchers from several disciplines (Crosby, 1984; Epstein, 1983; Thoits, 1983; Verbrugge, 1982). Thoits (1983) reported a positive correlation between the number of roles a person occupies and psychological well-being.

Men's participation in domestic work has slightly increased in recent years. However their contribution to domestic work is likely to be 'helping' rather than 'sharing' tasks and this reflects the ideology that men are still perceived to be the main providers

(Brannen et al 1994). Despite working full-time, women are often expected to meet domestic commitments. According to Pleak (1977) boundaries between work and family role are asymmetrically permeable (i.e. opposite in direction for male and female). The work roles of men are permitted to intrude on family roles, but not the reverse. On the other hand, the family roles of women are permitted to intrude on work roles but not the reverse. In medicine, the effects of marriage and family are the opposite for male and female doctors (Uhlenberg and Cooney, 1990).

There is some evidence that conflicting demands from work and family can be stressful (Lewis and Cooper, 1988). Working women are affected by stressors which are common to both sexes, but they experience additional stressors which are unique to women (Hendrix et al 1994). In an article in GP newsletter Pinders (1997) pointed out that women's relationship to time is shaped by age, class, race and position in the labour market. Time is not experienced equally. More often women's time is other people's time and although these patterns are changing women still do tasks to release others for 'more important work' (Davies, 1989). Heins et al (1977) found that women doctors spend 90% as much time in medical practice as men doctors while tending to assume direct responsibility for home and family, therefore, they have the added burden of trying to balance the demands imposed by both sides. An interview study by Turner, Tippett and Raphael (1994) found that the women doctors with children had considerable stress due to competing priorities of time for spouse, family and career. These women reported a sense of guilt about relegating child care to others despite their belief that good quality care had no deleterious effect.

Women doctors reduce their career aspirations due to marital reasons and family responsibility (Firth-Cozens, 1990). The experiences of 11 women, in an interview study found that women are more likely to support their spouses' career when planning work location and job applications than vice versa (Turner, Tippet and Raphael, 1994). Many studies show that women doctors take most of the responsibility for household management and childcare, alongside with their career demands (Fine, 1981). They work fewer hours and earn less income (Williams, Pierre and Vayda, 1993).

Women doctors' stress

Since the mid-seventies the gender specific problems of women doctors have been addressed. This may be due to the increasing number of women in medicine (Bickel, 1988). Although many of the sources of stress associated with medical practice are general, it may be possible that women doctors experience stressors that are unique to their gender. For example, studies found that prejudice against women in the profession, lack of role models and role conflict were the primary stressors for women doctors (Bowman and Allen, 1990; Cartwright, 1987). Evidence suggests that male and female doctors carry out different roles within their job, e.g. 'psychological' versus the 'clinical' role (Simpson and Grant, 1991). Chambers and Campbell (1996) compared male and female general practitioners, job satisfaction and professional commitments and found that female general practitioners derive more satisfaction from relations with patients than their male counterparts. A number of studies of doctors found that due to professional socialisation, male and female doctors have similar values and behaviour (Gross, 1997; Maheux et al 1988). Recently from a questionnaire study, it was found that both male and female general practitioners were moderately satisfied with their job, i.e. there was no significant differences between male and female general practitioners in the job satisfaction scale (Rout, 1999). Multivariate Analysis disclosed these job stressors (time pressure, working environment and career achievements) were predictive of high levels of job dissatisfaction for both male and female general practitioners (Rout, 1999).

In a comparative study in the USA, Gross (1997) indicated that although male and female doctors felt pressured by the amount of time demanded by their profession, female had the additional pressure of family obligations. Male doctors were most stressed by relationships with patients, threat of malpractice and inability to cure, whereas female doctors were more concerned about the responsibility inherent in the doctor's role. The author concluded that although doctors have several similar attitudes due to their professional socialisation their responses to the pressure of medical practice are also directed by sex-role socialisation.

Medicine is acknowledged as a high status and highly paid occupation. Therefore it could be argued that female doctors have greater resources than some other occupations (i.e. paid less and lower status) for coping with problems originating from work and home conflict. For example, they can provide domestic help and quality childcare which can help them to concentrate fully on their profession. Swanson et al (1998) conducted a study to find out the difference between male and female doctors' stress due to the interface between home and work. The finding suggests that increased domestic role complexity and parenthood in particular, are related to reduced occupational working hours on call, but increased time spent on domestic work for women doctors. For male doctors, in comparison with non-parents, working hours and time on call are increased, and time spent on housework or childcare is also increased, but less than for female doctors. Home demands have a greater impact on female doctors whereas work demands have a greater impact on male doctors. Female doctors had less satisfaction with their spouses' contribution to domestic work suggesting traditional patterns of domestic responsibilities. This finding was also reported by Lewis and Cooper's (1987) dual-career couples study.

As mentioned earlier, role strain is one of the main stressors for women. Women doctors find it difficult to fulfil their different role obligations, i.e. domestic responsibility and medical work. For example, in our previous study, conducted during 1987 in England, it was revealed that for female doctors the impact of the work-family interface was the most important stressor (Rout, 1989). Firth-Cozens (1987) reported that most frequent stressors for female junior doctors was conflict between career and personal life. Women carried major responsibility for home and family life. Other studies have suggested that home vs. work conflicts are damaging to health (Davidson and Cooper, 1984) and more and more married women are either divorcing, limiting their family size, or coping with both worlds at the expense of their physical and psychological health (Cooper, 1982).

Women doctors had a four fold increased risk of suicide compared to others in social class 1 (Richings et al 1986) and 46%

of a sample of women house officers fulfilled the criteria of clinical depression (Firth-Cozen, 1990). The results of a Norwegian study indicate that health complaints were significantly more frequent in female doctors (Aasland et al 1997). Other studies also have linked work/home stress with psychological ill health and job satisfaction in doctors (e.g. Firth-Cozens, 1987; Nadelson et al 1979) and female doctors are more likely to divorce than their male counterparts (Sandlin, 1990). In Myers (1984) study 13 of the 16 husbands of the women doctors came from traditional backgrounds with the belief that capable career women do not have emotional needs. As a result the dependency needs of the wives were ignored. Other problems include intimacy and sexuality (Myers, 1984).

Conflict between career and personal life was one of the most important and frequent stressors for female doctors (Cartwright, 1987, Cooper et al 1989, Firth-Cozen, 1990). Other authors point out that women are traditionally expected to assume direct responsibility for their own parents and husbands which is an added source of stress during the medical career (Nadelson and Notman, 1983). In addition, women doctors were particularly stressed by the pressures and desire to be with their children and other dual career issues.

A comparative study of consultants and general practitioners showed that females had less occupational stress and greater job satisfaction overall than males (Swanson et al 1996). Our 1987 study revealed that female doctors were more satisfied in their job than their male counterparts and their mental health was better than male doctors (Rout, 1989). It was found from the same study that female general practitioners showed significantly higher Type A scores than female managers. Thus women who take up medicine as a career may be highly motivated.

Richardson and Burke (1993) studied 303 women physicians in Canada and found that time pressures and threat of litigation were major sources of stress. In addition, they reported that women who experienced high stress and low satisfaction were more likely to have negative views of the functioning of the health care system. Weisman and Teitelbaum (1987) found that married family physicians work fewer hours than married male physicians and women's work hours are more responsive to family circumstances than men's. Women work fewer professional hours when they are more involved in household and child-care responsibilities and when their husbands earn incomes similar to theirs, but the same effects are not present for men. Some studies suggest that female doctors face more job-related stress than do males in similar positions (Ducker, 1986, Coombs and Hovanessian, 1988). Some research suggests few differences in female and male medical students' self evaluation of medical skills (Grant and DuRoss, 1984, Leserman, 1981). Simpson and Grant (1991) found no differences by gender in the types or magnitude of stressors experienced by male and female doctors. The authors explained this by saying that women and men enter medical school with gender systematic differences in perceived skills, but after medical school they show few differences.

In a sample of Canadian family doctors, Brown (1992) found that nearly two thirds of the sample (n=62) felt overloaded or overwhelmed by their multiple responsibilities as often as once per week. However, these women reported lower depression scores than other populations and the self esteem was similar to that of the other population. This result is consistent with a recent study that working mothers reported less depression than the non-working mothers (Rout et al 1997). Therefore the effects of employment on women's mental health have positive effects. These studies substantiate the argument of Bolger et al (1990) that 'alternate resources provided by multiple roles outweigh the stresses and help dampen their emotional effects'.

Our study

The following discussion presents the findings of our qualitative studies. The aim of these studies was to identify sources of stress among general practitioners, hospital doctors and their families. Our studies on stress among doctors in the UK have been going on since 1987 (Rout and Rout, 1993). The interview sample described here is part of the most recent series of studies and relates to 49 (36 male, 13 female) general practitioners in 1987, 25 (15 male and 10 female) general practitioners in 1992, and their families who were among the sample, who participated in our interviews. Altogether the sample consisted of 74 general practitioners. During 1995 and 1996 we interviewed 30 hospital consultants and 23 junior doctors and their families. The inclusion criteria were that the doctors be married, have children and currently practise medicine. The detailed analysis of male doctors, the spouses and children's interviews described elsewhere. The interviews were aimed at exploring personal and professional aspects of medicine, especially stress related to the job and possible overflow of stress into their family life. The sample of general practitioners was selected from a variety of practices, for example: solo v group, urban v rural and social mixed areas. The sample of consultants and junior doctors were selected by snowballing and networking. Their age range varied from 32 to 60 years. Confidentiality and anonymity of participants was assured. The interviews were tape recorded and took between 35 minutes and one hour. The tapes were transcribed and thematic analysis was carried out.

The interpretation of the results may not be accurate due to two reasons. First, qualitative methods have been criticised because of their subjectivity, second; one of the authors is a general practitioner and the other is a general practitioner's wife, which might have affected the content of the interviews. However, a qualitative approach was adopted since the aim was to gain an understanding of how doctors perceived and experienced stress.

Responses to questions about sources of stress were analysed to identify recurrent themes concerning sources of stress at work and at home. Only the stressors concerning female general practitioners will be discussed here.

They are as follows:

- role conflict/impact of work on family life
- emotional involvement
- work overload
- lack of support
- lack of time
- career stress
- communication difficulties.

Role conflict

Role conflict occurs due to the multiple role demands inherent in running a career, home and family. The stress is a product of conflict between the role of a woman and role of a doctor. Carrying out the traditional role of a mother and a spouse and a professional role in a satisfying way requires time and energy. One young female doctor who had joined a group practice recently was a typical example:

> When I took up the job I was told that I would be given priority for getting time off during my children's school holidays. But when one of my children fell ill I was not allowed to have time off. I was under severe pressure trying to finish the surgery to come home and look after my son.
>
> (GP, age 33)

The ability to separate home life from work can help to alleviate the effects of stress. On the other hand, most of the female consultants expressed that when on-call this separation strategy was impossible. One consultant claimed:

> It is difficult to separate home life from work life,........because mostly work spills over to home life when you are on-call.
>
> (Gynaecologist, age 53)

The two-career couples

Now-a-days many doctors' spouses are professionals, who derive pleasure and gratification from their work. Apart from this set of dual-career couples there is a special kind of group - dual-doctor marriage. There are enormous advantages in this type of marriage, for example they provide good education for the children, comfortable family home, other family needs social status and of course other material success. Both partners recognise the ability to empathise and share the pain associated with practice of medicine. However, there are several accompanying disadvantages in these marriages especially for women. The doctor's demands to the practice of medicine takes the priority over family and children. On-call duty, telephone calls and emergencies interrupt the family togetherness and closeness. The following quote illustrates this:

> When I am on-call I stay in the hospital accommodation away from my husband and children, sometimes more than 24 hours at a stretch, even longer during weekends. All I am able to do is to give them a ring if I am not too busy. That even does not happen very often. I do not have time for the family.
>
> (SHO, age 35)

When both husband and wife are professionals both may suffer from role strain. They try to do too much in too little time and forget about their own time together for talk and relaxation. Everyday tensions may spill into the marriage causing problems between the couple. We interviewed a couple who were suffering from role strain.

Dr Smith was 42 years old and a general practitioner in an urban group practice in the North West region of England. Mrs Smith was 39 years old and a University professor. They had been married for 15 years and had two children (14 and 12 years old) In addition to their professional jobs and looking after two children, both were active working in the community. Dr Smith worked five days a week in the surgery, did a clinic in a local hospital, attended research group meetings and PGEA (Post Graduate Education Allowance) meetings regularly, went to commissioning meetings, and took the children to music lessons and tennis lessons. Mrs Smith also worked five days a week, belonged to several committees (which took up lots of her time), did some volunteer work for the local community, attended all of her children's music and athletic events in school and outside, supervised their homework, and ran the house on her own, and was writing a book which she had to finish within two months. She was also grieving the loss of her mother who died a month before. She told us:

> I cannot cope with these any more. Too many things to do. It is ridiculous that even I don't have time to cry over my mother's death.
>
> (GP, age 42)

Emotional involvement

Some women general practitioners find it difficult to distance themselves from patients. They find it particularly hard to break bad news to the patients and their relatives. As a female general practitioner illustrated:

> I find it extremely difficult to tell the true diagnosis to a patient whom I've known very well for many years who is suffering from an incurable disease...contact with these kind of patients gives me anxiety which eventually leads to complete emotional exhaustion.
>
> (GP, age 38)

Work overload

Although both male and female doctors are affected, to some extent, by work overload and conflict from multiple roles, the burden of family responsibility falls on female doctors. The situation is often exacerbated by the expectations of the partners for the female general practitioners to work long hours in the work place. Domestic commitments and parental responsibilities may be a deciding factor for female general practitioners to work part-time. However, the ever increasing volume of work in the surgery and lack of contribution of the spouse to the housework may cause stress. As a female general practitioners said:

> I am a part-time partner (in the surgery) so I should do less work than the others. Everyone wants to push more work on to me, thinking that I am a woman and can't protest against anything. I have to fight in more than one corner at work and at home. Although I work hard in the surgery, I have to be in the kitchen to feed the family after getting back from work. I feel so exhausted that I have no time to do anything for myself.
>
> (GP, age 41)

Lack of support

On the whole, the women general practitioners we have spoken to believe that their husbands were not understanding. This is illustrated by a female general practitioner:

> Although we both are doctors my job gets underestimated. I am unable to attend any meeting or conference. He always gives priority to his work, however small it may be.
>
> (GP, age 37)

In some cases both partners do not like to talk about the problems and usually do not express negative feelings openly. This may be due to being afraid of making the situation unpleasant. By doing this the gap between the couple may become wider and wider and the trust in the relationship may be damaged.

For example, as a woman general practitioner working in a single handed practice commented:

> I do not have any feelings towards him anymore. I do still love him but the way he behaves .... I am hurt. I do not have any intimacy. He is not open, does not discuss anything. This has been going on since a year.
>
> (GP, age 42)

Doctor wife, non-doctor husband

Almost all of the significant literature available on married doctors considers the traditional male-doctor, female non-doctor-wife partnership and there are very few studies examining female doctors and male non-doctor husbands, or indeed other types of stable relationships. Some women doctors complained that their non-doctor husbands do not understand their work responsibility.

A female doctor expressed her dissatisfaction with her husband's attitude towards her work and family life:

> My husband is uncooperative. Sometimes we have meals at different times which is not kind of family life. In the evening sometimes I keep the meal ready for my son when he comes from school he can have it, other times he has to sort himself out. My husband works in a nearby city. When he comes home he will have his meal. I go home quite late, then I have a cold meal. Sometimes if they remember to warm up my meal in the microwave, I will have it then.
>
> (GP, age 45)

Similarly another female general practitioner commented:

> It was an arranged marriage. He wanted to marry a doctor. So he knew the lifestyle of a doctor. He has voluntarily got involved sharing housework, shopping and helping me in the practice. Though, being a typical Asian husband he wouldn't like to help. I mean he wouldn't mind that he is helping but it will come out in another form that I have helped her such and such time, and I do all the shopping. Deep in his mind the woman's role is doing everything. You are doing all these jobs, but still he is the boss. ....When I am really feeling ill, he will not understand that........They (all Indian men) have got a feeling which they won't say directly but deep inside in their minds... they are helping, but other times they will tell you something which will make you aware that you are not the same. You are doing all these jobs, but still he's the boss.
>
> (GP, age 40)

Some women doctors' husbands are comfortable with their gender-role change. For example, one woman doctors' husband was a taxi driver when they were married. Now he is a full-time homemaker. He is very happy about his role. As Dr. Rose said:

> My husband looks after my children when I am working. We both sat down and decided this is the best way for both of us. He is very happy in raising the children. I do a lot of reading and writing on top of my clinical duty. He does not complain. I am very pleased we took the decision this way.
>
> (GP, age 34)

Another woman general practitioner who also had a teaching commitment expressed her satisfaction about the arrangements they had for their home and children responsibilities. Her husband was a chiropodist who worked part-time in a group practice of five general practitioners. He was happy to take most of the responsibilities for children and the house. Dr Saunders was proudly expressing to me:

> My husband is very co-operative. He takes care of the children, cooks the dinner and very sympathetic towards my work. I take work home because I do some research and teaching. My surgery commitment is less than others. I have more paperwork.
>
> (GP, age 43)

This shows that the couple had good communication and mutual respect for each other. Although in today's society professional couples expect egalitarian relationship in their marriages they may find it hard to adjust to, due to their traditional thinking rooted in their early developmental years. These roles may be perceived as deviant to the outside world due to the cultural norm in our society.

The sample contained only seven non-doctor husbands and the information from the interview was very little. Surprisingly non-doctor husbands were very supportive as they claimed and were very proud of their wives' careers.

> I am very proud of my wife. She is doing a responsible job. As she earns more than me we decided that I should stay at home and look after the children
>
> (Chiropodist, age 42)

Lack of time

The areas of conflict for doctors and spouses are lack of time for children and time together. The stress most frequently reported was guilt about having very little time and attention given to their children, and fatigueresulting from working long hours. They felt deprived of time for themselves. The wives of male doctors took over the responsibility for housekeeping and child care, but the women doctors handled these on their own.

As a woman GP said:

> I do not get any time for myself. I am always on the go. My work never ends even if I finish the surgery. Another shift starts at home. This is different for my male colleagues. They have time to rest at home when their wives look after their children and home.
>
> (GP, age 33)

Career stress

Sometimes women doctors suppress and deny their ambitions and dreams to become consultants. They sacrifice their career for their husband's career and for their family.

> I am just a community physician now. I was a very bright student during my university life. Due to my husband's career I suppressed my wishes to become a consultant. My marriage and my children came first. My husband is a consultant who is very committed to his work. Both of us cannot pursue demanding careers. One has to sacrifice.
>
> (Community Physician, age 38)

Women doctors may find it difficult to return to work after a career break, especially in such a fast-changing field as medicine. They may have to return to lower status jobs due to unavailability of retraining. As a doctor in our interview sample expressed:

> Now I am a practice manager in a group practice. After such a long time gap I came back to work. I lost my confidence in treating patients. I had to teach myself computer skills. Still then I am not confident. I am not very happy right now. One day I hope to go back to medicine otherwise it is a waste of resources.
>
> (GP, age 45)

Communication difficulties

Some married women doctors in our sample expressed unhappiness due to the lack of communication with their spouses at home and with colleagues in the workplace. These women could not assert themselves at home in stating their needs and demands to their spouses. They gave different reasons for this. The following example illustrates this:

Dr. White was a full-time general practitioner in an urban group practice. After the day's work she used to come home, cook the dinner and lay the table for her husband and two teenage boys. One evening she was late because of a number of home visits. She wanted to make sure the family had the evening meal. She rang home while visiting the last patient and was angry when she found out that her husband was waiting for her to come and cook the dinner for them. She narrated this event:

> I felt so angry I could not speak to him. I stopped the car on the way, cried and then wiped my tears. Then bought four meals from ASDA (supermarket). After arriving home I put the food bag on the dining table and went upstairs to change. Until I came back downstairs they were sitting and watching TV. I was expecting my husband to put the food on plates on the dining table. I was speechless. How can people be like that expecting the woman to do everything.
>
> (GP, age 46)

Problems faced by women doctors do not stop at home. In the workplace they have similar kinds of problem where they cannot assert themselves.

For example a woman GP explained:

> I have been in this practice for 12 years. Whenever we have a practice meeting I don't have a chance to put forward my views. All four partners are male. They just make their points and take it for granted all these are approved by me. Sometimes I bring these problems home and cry, but nobody knows the matter. My husband is not very sympathetic. He always advises me to speak

for myself but does not know the root cause. Then we have argument at home for this.

(GP, age 38)

Husband and wife arguments becomes an everyday way of life when they find themselves incompatible. They feel unable to communicate with each other. The following example explains this:

Dr Patel is an established general practitioner. She did not have any problem getting into general practice, rather she was offered partnership from several practices. She had a problem deciding which practice to join because she did not want to practise near her ex-husband's practice area. When I interviewed her she became emotional. She told me about her disastrous marriage. She said:

> I fell in love with him in the first year of medical school. Being in the same year we did a lot of things together. I mean course work for the college and other things outside the college. I was so much in love with him that everything looked colourful to me. We decided to get married in the second year of medical school. All was well until we both got into vocational training in General Practice. We worked in the same hospital and lived together. Everything was fine until I developed a gynaecological problem. I had to be admitted to the hospital for several days. On discharge from the hospital I noticed him completely changed. I was suspicious that there was something going on. He hardly came to see me in the ward. He said he had been on call to cover a colleague. We had several arguments everyday. Later he expressed that he had lost his feelings for me. I was devastated and was so angry that I left him. We met on several occasions during the training year in General Practice but never spoke to each other.
>
> He joined a local practice. I was not quite sure which geographical area to choose. After a while I ended up joining a practice in the same area. I was told that he has had affairs with nurses and young lady representatives while we were married. Since divorce, I met a handsome non-medic and married him. We have two children and we are both very happy.

(GP, age 36)

This couple's marriage ended in divorce, probably because of a combination of factors including their commitment to their relationship at a very young age or may be due to lack of communication between them.

Another example:

Dr Charles was married to Samantha who worked in the same hospital as a Senior House Officer in psychiatry. Later she became a registrar in psychiatry in another hospital, and Dr Charles pursued his aim to become a plastic surgeon. For a while they managed to live together, although they had to work in different hospitals. Surgical job for Dr Charles meant working erratic hours, whereas his wife enjoyed a fairly less demanding job. However, their social life began to lose its glitter.

Dr Charles said:

> I wanted to be a plastic surgeon. I really worked hard in surgery and you know how busy Senior House Officer's are. My wife wanted to make a career in psychiatry and worked towards it. I always had sympathy towards her thinking that she dealt with psychiatric patients who can drive people crazy and even make the doctor mad. By the time she came home she looked emotionally drained. I let her rest and do most of the work in the kitchen. During dinner I would sympathetically listen to her problems in dealing with difficult patients. But when it came to my side of the job pressure she never appreciated how hard it was for me to work in a busy surgical unit. I suppose after a while we became selfish by concentrating on our own careers and never appreciating each others difficulties. The feelings between us got rapidly diluted. I could not see any bright prospect in becoming a plastic surgeon and decided to get into general practice. She got a registrar's job in a hospital 200 miles from here and our relationship became million miles apart. We decided to divorce. I remarried two years later. My wife is a housewife and we are both very happy.
>
> (GP, age 35)

However, in spite of the stress, some women doctors have successfully integrated their home and work responsibilities. A lady doctor who was working in a hospital at the time of interview gave some positive comments on the understanding and arrangements at home. For example:

> Weekend is the only time when cooking is sorted out for the whole week. We eat together during the weekend. My husband and children are very understanding and supportive.
>
> (SHO, age 35)

Divorce

Multiple commitments to work, home and community prevent time for marriage for women in general. Men doctors deny the marital unhappiness. This is magnified by the pride of the women doctors who are in a profession where men have been in the domineering position for many many years. They usually delay in seeking help for marital problems. There are several problems in seeking help - for example, feeling of guilt and failure and self-image problems.

Although some women doctors' professional life is doing well, their family life especially marriage may be a failure. Those women doctors whose husbands initiate their divorce may feel abandoned. This is illustrated in the following example:

Dr Susan Wall was interviewed by me after she was divorced. She told me that her husband has abandoned her, she said:

> I am depressed, I have no interest in life. My husband left me for another younger woman. My self-esteem is low. I feel very ugly and unattractive. We have been married for twenty years and I have two boys. I left my boys with him for two months and stayed with my mother. My mother has been very helpful to me. I could not cope. Now I am trying very hard to live, but I cannot forget him. I feel abandoned, life is a burden for me now. I am taking anti-depressants regularly. I still do not know how I am surviving.
>
> (Registrar, age 49)

For other women doctors the family situation may be depressing but they do not like to be separated. For example:

> Although I do not have children I do not like to break the marriage. I have married him for life. I have to try to make the most of my

marriage, I am not happy in many situations, but I love him. I do not like to be on my own. Separation or divorce sounds frightening to me. My friends said to me few times that 'you have a good profession and you are good looking, why can't you think of a different life-style?' I gave a thought many times but it doesn't appeal to me.

(SHO, age 33)

Impact of divorced doctors on children

Children of divorced doctors may have negative feelings towards their parents. The negative feelings may be directed to one of the parents who initiated the divorce. In our study we interviewed a teenager, the son of a divorced doctor couple who was devastated by his parents separation. He was very upset and angry at his father because he initiated the divorce as he was seeing another younger woman. After the divorce his father moved in with the other woman. As this son of the doctor put it:

> I am very angry with my father, I can't tolerate the fact that he is in love with this woman who is 20 years younger than him. I feel my mother is humiliated at this age.
>
> (Boy, age 15)

Another child in a similar situation said:

> I don't like my dad anymore, I feel that he doesn't love me anymore. He loves his new wife's children. He is with them every holiday. I resent this. He is a very good doctor, but not a good father.
>
> (Girl, age 12)

We interviewed two more teenage children of a doctor couple who were going through divorce at that time. Their father was an anaesthetist and their mother a general practitioner. Both the children were in sixth form college (one 17 years and the other 18 years old). These children were spoilt with very expensive things (i.e. designer clothes, expensive game equipment, expensive toys). They stayed one week with mother and one with father. Both parents were living in the same town. Although they were getting everything they wanted, they were not happy children. For example:

> I am very unhappy about my parents separation. My friends are asking the reason. I am embarrassed about my mother's behaviour because she is living with this young man. She does not care about us. She does not ask how I feel.

(Girl, age 17)

On the other hand her brother was detached about the whole thing. He said he was happy about the divorce. He said:

> My parents never got on well. My father was always busy in the hospital and my mother was equally occupied in her work. Whenever they were at home they were arguing about very little things. I did not like the atmosphere. I am glad that they are separated. This should have happened long time before. My sister is very upset about this, but I am not.

(Boy, age 18)

Conclusions

The literature on gender differences in doctors is ambiguous (Gross, 1997). There is a lack of research on stress in women doctors in this country, especially on divorce, as this is a sensitive topic to discuss openly. The members of these doctors' families agreed to be interviewed, as I am a doctor's wife and a psychologist. Our qualitative research in this chapter addresses the issues of the stress in women doctors. Role strain and work overload reported in this chapter come as no surprise. This is described in both male and female doctors (Roesek, 1981; Rout and Rout, 1993). However, role strain for married female doctors may be more intense than their male counterparts. This is not specific to the women in medical profession but this is observed in women of other professions. Uhlenberg and Cooney (1990) reported that over 80% of married female doctors do the household shopping compared to only 2% of male doctors in Britain. Although women have jobs like men they are still expected to take full responsibility for domestic arrangements and childcare. However, personalities, needs and expectations of these women are unknown and how they are similar to and different from male doctors is also unknown. Nevertheless further studies are needed to address these issues. The purpose of the next chapter is to discuss stress affecting overseas doctors and their family members.

4 Overseas Doctors and Families

The aim of this chapter is to describe the problems, pressures and barriers faced by overseas qualified doctors, their wives and children. Overseas qualified doctors comprise 24 per cent of the medical workforce and this proportion is increasing (Dept. of Health, 1997). The majority of overseas doctors are qualified from non-EEA countries. Here the term overseas is used to include doctors whose primary qualification was acquired from South Asian countries (e.g. India, Pakistan, Bangladesh and Burma).

Stress in overseas doctors

Overseas doctors may face difficulties owing to their cultural background, limited registration, race discrimination and language difficulties. Tavistock clinic pilot study on young doctors found that overseas doctors struggle to get jobs in general medicine or surgery for which they see themselves as qualified (Hale and Hudson, 1992). Other difficulties include: accommodation, conflicts with consultants and staff, and lack of family support. In our previous nationwide study it was found that overseas qualified doctors had significantly greater pressure, more dissatisfaction in their job and more type A behaviour than their UK counterparts (Rout, 1989; Rout and Rout, 1993). Overseas qualified general practitioners were more stressed because of adverse publicity in the press and patients complaints than UK-qualified general practitioners (Rout and Rout, 1993).

Discrimination

Many of the overseas doctors experienced a different form of racism exhibited by white people (colleagues and patients). This was referred by some doctors as 'indirect systematic institutional racism'. Such behaviours and attitudes were displayed in the form of complaints and (adverse) publicity. The effect of this principally related to the ways in which overseas doctors were approached and treated by colleagues and patients. While the number of litigations against doctors rise rapidly they are likely to suffer from increasing stress. The overseas doctors in particular take this seriously as they think they are more prone to such complaints on account of discrimination. This was highlighted by many overseas doctors.

> However good I am, one cannot remove prejudice and racial discrimination from peoples minds. I have to be very careful of what I do because a slight error might bring my name on the front page of the local newspaper. No one will appreciate your good work but a minute mistake will take you to hell.
>
> We need to work twice as hard to please patients and to be accepted by the local colleagues. If mistakes are made they tend to be of less help in understanding it or sorting them out.
>
> Lot of us work in a constant fear of adverse publicity in the press and it is very demanding and stressful to prove to them that we are equally good and caring.

The medical trainings in the overseas countries are mainly clinical with no social orientation. Overseas doctors came to this country with the intention of receiving specialist training in order to become specialists in the hospitals but lack of scope has forced them into general practice (without much choice). Due to their ethnic background, fear of discrimination and lack of training in social skills they are compelled to work harder and faster in order to get parity with the UK qualified doctors. The following examples highlight the situations.

Dr Rana was a general practitioner. He had his life's ambition to build his career in hospital medicine hoping to be a consultant physician. He worked hard and passed his membership examination. Once he realised that his chances of becoming a consultant were rather remote he decided to get into general practice. He found that the set-up and the type of work carried out in general practice were totally different from he expected. He appeared to have lost interest in everything, cancelled his surgeries without giving prior notice, became irritable with patients and surgery staff. His wife complained that Dr Rana showed detached attitude towards her and the children. He did not sleep well and started getting up in the early hours of morning. He was not prepared to discuss his problem. Dr Rana was a non-smoker and liked an occasional drink but recently he started drinking heavily. His partners were worried about him and offered to discuss any help that he may need but he did not trust them. A few months later he suffered a nervous breakdown and resigned from his job.

Dr Ariya was working in a group practice in the North West of England. She thought that she was lucky to have a practice in her home town. She joined a group practice of three doctors and was initially happy for a year until the circumstances appeared to be different from what she had initially perceived. Her senior partners started to push more and more work towards her, which she perceived as unfair and discriminatory. She said: "Because I am an Asian woman my partners tend to push more and more work on me". She tried her best to cope with the workload but began to feel tired. She was unable to relax and felt undervalued. Her appetite became poor and she lost weight. Her patients commented about her weight loss and withdrawn appearance, which made her feel even worse. She felt depressed and had to stay off work for several months. After she saw her general practitioner she was admitted to hospital with severe depression. After a while she recovered from her illness but decided not to go back to work. She is now at home. She told us that her parents were disappointed because they felt that so many years of medical training had been wasted. However, they were happy to see that she had recovered from depression.

Lack of support

One of the most common problems of overseas doctors and their wives is isolation and loneliness. The couple miss their families, friends and culture. Because of cultural differences overseas doctors might find it difficult to socialise with their British medical colleagues. In case of problems they seek support from their spouses which may not be adequate and puts pressure on the marriage.

Dr Sinha, who qualified in India, was a general practitioner in an urban group practice. He explained to us the following:

> Once one of my patients made a complaint against me for professional negligence after her mother died of pneumonia. This case was referred to the Health Authority for a formal hearing. Although I had tendered my best possible medical care to her mother the thought of facing the formal hearing was very stressful. My partners (in the workplace) offered no help and my wife didn't understand the gravity of the problem. I had several sleepless nights and went through agony for many days. During that period I wished that my parents and other family members were here to give me support. Time like this is very painful. You need your family.
>
> (GP, age 42)

Dr Ahmed and her husband were both general practitioners. They did not practise together but they both worked under the same Health Authority. Dr Ahmed was an extrovert but her husband was just the opposite. She was involved in medical politics and remained away from home quite often. Her two children were attached to their father. She developed a tendency to get away from the practice as much as she could. Unfortunately she was charged with professional negligence after the death of one of her patients. The case went on for several months. She went through a very stressful period. She did not get any support from her husband or her children. When we interviewed her she said:

> I have a family who do not show any sympathy towards me. My husband never supported me during my difficult period.
>
> (GP, age 43)

In our study the average pressure score for overseas general practitioners, in response to the statement 'lack of emotional support from spouse', was significantly higher than the UK-qualified general practitioners (Rout and Rout, 1993). Spouses of overseas qualified general practitioners often have the disadvantage of not having their parents or close relations in this country. Their husbands are the main support, perhaps the only social support to their families. The busy doctor deprives his spouse of her share of attention and care because of his out-of-hours commitments. In a study, Elliot (1978) found that the doctors' heavy workload meant that their wives were taking on the role of father/husband as well as their own wife/mother role, and were exhausted and overwhelmed by the dual responsibility. This heavy burden on doctors' wives reflects in lack of emotional support for their husbands, hence causing stress in doctors.

Separation and divorce

Although Asian families are fairly stable than many other groups in the UK (White and Woolet, 1981) separation and divorce may not be uncommon among overseas doctors in the modern world. Overseas doctors and their spouses usually do not seek help when they have any marital problem. Although they go to see their general practitioner they do not report the conflict at home due to the cultural restrictions. This is also found from a study on depression that depressed Asian patients expressed their symptoms in somatic terms to their general practitioner (Rout and Rout, 1996). They usually struggle with the problem by themselves. When the problem becomes complicated and intense the couple may split. We interviewed a consultant whose wife went back to India after many unpleasant incidences. Eventually the marriage ended in divorce.

> After working in this country for some years, I went to India to get married. It was arranged by my parents. I liked the girl as she was good looking, educated and came from an upper class family. After the marriage she came here with me. I had three days leave still left before resuming my work. We had a good time during those days. Problems started when I went back to work. I was working long hours and was not able to come home for lunch. She was on her own all day. The moment I reach home in the evening she wanted

> to go out to the cinema or shopping. She didn't realise that I would be tired after the long hours of work in the hospital. I expected the evening meal to be ready for us but she wanted to eat out. As she came from a rich family things were done for her at home. She was not used to doing things for herself or others. She never took any responsibility in India. I thought that after marriage she would be responsible for maintaining the domestic affair. This never happened and the marriage did not work. We were not able to communicate with each other in same frequency. She rang her mother to take her to India and she went back to India with her mother. She never came back and the marriage ended in divorce.
>
> (Consultant, age 46)

Divorce not only affects the family life but also the work life.

Dr Gopal was a full-time partner in a group practice of three doctors. She was sincere and hard working. Both of her partners exploited her and made her work hard. She carried on working but at a price to her own physical and psychological health and to her marriage. While going through a difficult period in her practice, her marriage ended in divorce which added to her stress. Her two grown up children decided to live with their father making her feel lonely and abandoned. She was unable to work effectively in the practice. Her partners dissolved the partnership and as a result she had to leave the practice. She started a single handed practice in the same area. There were several hurdles before she could set-up her practice. Although she was without the hassles of partners she experienced difficulty in working on her own. Two years after starting her own practice she resigned from the practice and has remained unemployed until recently. She explained:

> I felt tired all the time. I felt isolated from my patients, partners and the surgery staff. I spent less time in listening to my patients and I developed a habit of writing prescriptions before the patients finished talking about their problems. I treated some patients like my enemies. I didn't feel like giving advice to patients on the telephone and didn't like it when there was requests for visiting patients at their homes. My children pointed out to me that I was irritable while talking to patients on the telephone. I felt that there was nobody that I could talk to about my problems, even my husband was never supportive. Sadly our marriage ended in divorce

and my practice partnership was dissolved. Although I started my own practice and felt that there was no interference from partners, I was not able to cope with the surgery. I drank more alcohol than I ever did before. I still find difficult to get a good night sleep. I feel totally exhausted.

(GP, age 43)

Problems of overseas doctors' wives

Community pressure

In Asian culture the community and culture tend to play a significant role in personal and domestic activities. Due to cultural pressure a wife has to take most of the domestic responsibilities. The community criticises the wife if the husband helps in household jobs. Not surprisingly the wife has to be very careful about this.

> I feel harassed because outside people don't understand. They think that the husband is doing such a lot for his wife and his wife is not satisfied. Why is that? I am not saying that they do it purposefully. I think it is deeply rooted in the culture.
>
> (Registrar's wife, SHO, age 39)

> I think it is deep-rooted from generation to generation. They (men) have changed a lot because they are in a different country. If they were there, back in India, they wouldn't help at all. They are helping because they are forced to. My husband didn't do anything for my child. I have only one child. My mother used to help me. Everything should be fifty-fifty in these situations.
>
> (SHO's wife, SHO, age 38)

Lack of support

A doctor's wife with two children expressed that even if she didn't need the money for the family she wanted to work to keep her occupied. Her doctor husband didn't approve her working and didn't support her.

> I never expected to do anything, so life was very very hard because of being married to a doctor. He was never there to help me. So my

life was like having two jobs in my life, one is at home and one is outside. And I wanted to carry on with work. Physically it has been hard. But that's the way I am now I think I just do it. Now I always put my family first even my career and I think to a certain extent my career suffered, I think I suffered more than my career. I had been working up till 2 O'clock for school work but family didn't suffer at all. My husband didn't want me to work because financially he never needs my help, he can maintain all of us but I wanted to work because I have the education and I also felt bored at home. I suppose I needed stimulus for my intellect and I was prepared to work hard so that I could get it. I bought things for us, things for children, things that were not essential in the family.

(Consultant's wife, teacher, age 56)

Isolation

Another doctor's wife kept herself extremely busy, so that she would not feel lonely without her husband's company.

> I am the president of the Indian Women's Association this year and a member of the Classical Musical Society - Member of Manchester Indian Association, Bengali Cultural association and Religious Association of Merseyside and member of England Um.... Anything you name it I am in it, that's how I think I keep myself occupied.
>
> (Consultant's wife, teacher, age 50)

Doctors' wives who are housewives experience more isolation than working women on account of less contact with the outside world.

> I feel lonely, isolated, depressed most of the time. My husband is busy in his work. I am on my own all day in my house. When he comes home he is tired. I do not want to give him all my problems. I try to adjust - be good - make the dinner and have dinner together. I watch TV a lot. Sometimes it is boring. I have no one here. I always think of going for a walk, but I don't like to go on my own. When I came here 'he' (referring to husband) was working in a hospital and there were a lot of Asian doctors' wives. We used to go for walks wearing Indian clothes. I miss that now. My mum rang from India saying start something new, studying ... doing a

> course, otherwise your mental condition won't stay healthy. I have been thinking to take up a course in a nearby college. During the day when my husband is not at home I could go to college for couple of hours to keep me occupied and also I could make some friends. But this has not been materialised. I am very attached to my daughter, I miss her so much. She rings me regularly telling me to start something in adult education centre. I should start enquiring now. When my son and daughter come home for holiday I am very happy. Cooking in the kitchen all the time. They bring friends. They stay with us. I start cooking in the morning for breakfast, then for lunch and then for dinner. I enjoy this but sometimes this is too much. Cooking all the time gets monotonous.
>
> (GP's wife, age 49)

> Nowadays I accompany my husband when he does his housecalls. This is not very exciting but better than sitting at home.
>
> (GP's wife, age 45)

Another doctors' wife felt isolated even if she has three young children to look after. She said:

> During the day I get bored - do a bit of housework - watch TV in the kitchen - morning and lunchtime. I suppose it (TV) is always on. I am putting on weight so much. I feel depressed at times and eat and eat and eat.
>
> (GP's wife, age 40)

But on the contrary she admits that she feels happy after school and during the evening.

> I enjoy my children's company. I drop them at school and pick them up from school. I look at my youngest one's homework, give him bath, teach him lots of things. With my older ones I talk to them after they finish their home work. I attend to their school functions. My husband is always out. I miss him very much. At the same time I do not like to go out with him during evenings because I do not like to leave my children with anybody.
>
> (GP's wife, age 40)

This shows that this lady is very much attached to her children that she could sacrifice the evening out with her husband. This might be a problem in future when her children go to university. She will be obviously lost. She would not know what to do with her time unless she plans for it now.

Similarly another doctor's wife said:

> I have some friends here but I miss my own family. It is impossible to go to India every year now. It is expensive now which we cannot afford. I miss lots of things. When I am on my own I think about my home in India.
>
> (GP's wife, age 41)

Discrimination

One doctor's wife had problem at work stemming from discrimination and prejudice, but she did not want to express it at home. She thought that her husband would not support her. She said:

> She (the headmistress) was being very prejudiced and I found it very hard to take because in a primary school it's very difficult to stand up against the Head, because everybody believes the Head. If you want to keep your job you do as you're told. Race Relation Board in Manchester, somehow found out, and asked me would I like to do anything more about it. If I would have taken it to court or something like that I would be labelled and it would be hard for me. I came across many prejudices, a lot of racism and sexism. I was a soft target. I didn't dare to go and complain at home because my husband's comment would be who asked you to work, as he felt he was insulted through me ..... It was very stressful and you couldn't tell anybody which was the main thing. I mean if you did you didn't get much sympathy for it really.
>
> (Consultant's wife, teacher, age 56)

The overseas doctors' wives communicated that their husbands' problems were caused by their race rather than their professions.

> He had to try harder than white doctors to get to the top. We have a good house in a good area and we have better education for my

children. My children are exceptionally bright, but in the back of your mind you think that you are different and discrimination is inevitable.

(Consultant's wife, age 37)

Lack of communication

Lack of communication between husband and wife was a common theme for doctor couples.

> When Abdul became director of his medical services, he invited more and more people to our house. This was not for a drink or cup of tea, but for a proper dinner. Sometimes I had to entertain 40 to 50 people in one evening. I was shattered at the end of the party. Don't get me wrong, I loved every minute of it, but I needed some kind of help. Abdul never knew what was prepared for the dinner. He has too little time for all these.

(GP's wife, age 35)

Another geriatrician's wife said:

> He comes home after five o'clock, talks to me for one minute, then off to the golf club. At times I get mad at him because of his addiction. He loves golf madly, he is hooked.

(Consultant's wife, age 38)

> I used to have social life when my child was little and I used to work part time. But nowadays I am shattered when I finish work. So I request my husband to attend to social gatherings many a time. The pressure of work is such a lot. I haven't finished all this paperwork yet (as I was interviewing her. There are times when I am too shattered and I need a little bit of rest - I find that if they (my husband and my children) are out of the house I can lie down a bit. Whereas at other times the family is demanding on me, especially my husband. He wants this, that and the other, why isn't the cooking done. why isn't ..... Why do you want to lie down all the time etc. So if they are socialising I have my time. I need to lie down, maybe read my own book sometimes - just to cut off from the world. I like to read something in Indian which reminds me of home, my family (in India) or something.

(GP's wife, age 36)

The following case study depicts lack of communication between a couple resulting in a marriage without love instead of a divorce. However, this is owing to a calculated decision of the wife for the sake of their children.

Dr Biswas and his wife are from Indian background. They were married 20 years ago without knowing each other previously as it was an arranged marriage. Things were rosy for a year or so until the arrival of their (unplanned) baby. This was a blow to Mrs Biswas's ambition for higher studies and building a career although it did not affect her determination. She took more and more responsibility at home while Dr Biswas spent more time in the surgery. He maintained his attitude of superiority and took it for granted that there was no need for him to take any domestic responsibility. The domestic atmosphere appeared cloudy when Mrs Biswas started her university education as planned before her pregnancy. She found it extremely strenuous both physically and mentally to continue full-time education and have all the domestic responsibility. She was young and energetic and therefore managed with her determination and devotion. However, she could not achieve her grades in her examinations as expected.

The couple continued to remain married and Mrs Biswas moved on her career and completed her PhD and got a full-time job as a university lecturer. By then they had their second child. Both professionals had different commitments and responsibilities. As they discovered that there are difficulties in continuing in a full-time job and looking after children both developed a tendency to shift responsibilities and began to argue for simple things, even sometimes for no reason. They both were uncompromising and would not budge an inch. These episodes occurred frequently and the arguments became more intense. Dr Biswas wanted to avoid these confrontational situations and preferred to spend more time with his patients and in the office. Both of them remained on different wave lengths and there was less and less sensible communication between them. Both decided to keep confrontational situations away from their children but the children could not avoid noticing the tension between the parents.

I try to avoid the situation, keep quiet most of the time but you cannot hide the emotion all the time. I do not get any support from him. I have nobody here. I try to live for my children. My dream has been shattered.

(Registrar's wife, University Lecturer, age 32)

Mrs Biswas's experience being a doctor's wife in the UK turned out to be totally different to her previous perception. She would have felt isolated and depressed if she did not have a career and is now going through severe stress and strain as a full-time professional and gets no support from her husband physically or mentally. She has regrets for leaving India because her dream of luxurious life in England has proven to be totally unattainable.

Problems of overseas doctors' children

This section presents the reflection of Asian doctors' children on their family life. The content of this section provides only partial accounts of the Asian doctors' children's perspectives. A great deal has been omitted from the interviews because some of the statements were considered personal. I gave them assurance about the anonymity of the interview and promised them not to publish the bits they stated as personal. Although there were a number of similarities between the experiences of family life of these doctors' children there were several striking differences between them. These were probably due to their religion (Muslim vs. Hindu), age (younger vs. older), sex (male child vs. female child), and family constitution (nuclear vs. wider family network). As a consequence, the contrasting experiences were perhaps a reflection of a combination of all these factors as well as their individual perspectives and experiences of being an Asian doctor's child. Thus, just as British society as a whole is pluralistic, Asian communities have differences as well as similarities between them. What is apparent is that although there may exist unity and solidarity among culturally diverse and ethnically distinctive groups, it isn't possible to make any broad generalisations about members of Asian cultures on account of the existence of heterogeneity. The present research is less concerned with uncovering religious differences and more concerned with understanding the family experiences of Asian doctors' children living within a British context. Although there has been some research into the experience of Asian family life in Britain (Anwar, 1981; Kitwood, 1983; Westwood and Bhachu, 1988), none have looked into Asian doctors' children's experience.

The social-cultural background of the researcher (often white middle class) can play an important part in setting the research agenda, guiding the interviews and managing the relationship between interviewer and interviewee. Dilworth-Anderson et al (1993) have highlighted the role researcher's value have in shaping research into family life. They stress that care needs to be taken, particularly in work with culturally diverse families, so that the cultural integrity of the families studied is maintained intact. Attention to the 'cultural landscape' (Dilworth-Anderson et al 1993) and the different cultural realities is especially pertinent in the study of Asian doctors' children's experiences of family life. It would be very easy for an insensitive interviewing style to strip away children's confidence in expressing their own cultural norms, beliefs, attitudes and behaviours. It is with this in mind that I decided, as an Asian doctor's wife, to take on the task of interviewing Asian doctor's children. By being aware of cultural value issues, and by originating from a similar background, I hoped that the children would feel able to open up and talk freely to me about their family experiences. I knew them previously through doctors' families social gatherings. These interviews went extremely well.

Naman was 11 years old at the time of the interview. His father (aged 50) was a Consultant Physician in a local hospital and owned a private nursing home as well as some properties for rental. His mother (aged 42) was a housewife but spent much of her time caring for his sister (Nazia) who had a chronic lung disorder. At the time of interview, Nazia was in hospital and while awaiting a lung transplant had to spend a great deal of her time there. His father was busy most of the time in the hospital and looking after his nursing home. In terms of his immediate nuclear family, Naman was very much aware of their status within the Muslim community as well as within the English community. He felt proud to be the son of a medic and described his family background as privileged.

> I like a good home, a very big home like a mansion. I like it to be big. You've got television, you can watch television, you've got computer, you've got satellite, you know like SKY, all the SKY channels. You've got a Walkman you can listen to music and .. I like it to have a big garden to play in, and have slides and swings. I like it to have bushes, you know...I like getting the fruit out of the trees to eat. I like going to the forest (referring to his back garden) to play with my friends. Most of my friends are doctors' children like me.

Like his father he wanted to have a medical career.

> We go to hospital together, like I see what my dad's doing in hospital...When I grow up I would like to be a doctor like my dad, do medicine, like to be a consultant. Yeah, and I like to do medicine, you know, go in a hospital like my dad here in Chorley hospital. I'd like to own, like, Manchester hospital, or Bolton Hospital or you know, Great Ormond Street Hospital, one of them hospitals.

In Asian families parents and children communicate less often and less with each other. This is most likely due to the generation gap and the existence of intergenerational conflicts between the parents and their children. However, such conflicts were only minor for Naman as he felt secure with the Asian family structure imposing stability, networks and a sense of belonging. On the other hand Biny (girl, aged 15) was restricted by her parents to go out and socialise with her friends. She said:

> My parents do not like me to go out with my English friends so often. If I am allowed to go they have certain rules that I have to obey. Not to do this and not do that.

The main problems for Biny were experiencing culture conflicts, an identity crisis, and bicultural socialisation with no equal balance. It is often assumed that as the children grow up in multiethnic societies they experience identity crisis and feel themselves split between two cultures i.e. the culture of their parents and the host community (Kitwood, 1983). This is because rather than children making a compromise between the two cultures, they maybe forced to experience self-alienation and feel "suspended between both worlds" (Modgil, 1986). Naman was integrated in his own Muslim community who were in a similar position where he did not feel any different than his peers. He was happy to follow his culture, religion and tradition; such attitudes to the joint/extended family are popular among Asians and preferred by those who've had experience of it and enjoyed it.

Several authors assert that many young Asians in the UK affirm Asian or Islamic values and adopt Asian customs (Anwar, 1981, Kitwood, 1983, Stopes-Roe and Cochrane, 1990, Westwood and Bhachu, 1988). Naman's views are in accord with findings reported by Ballard and Ballard (1979), that it is perhaps an overgeneralisation that young Asians are likely to suffer from culture conflicts due to the wide range of complex personal experiences and the assumption that there is a straightforward clash between East and West, an either/or situation. Instead in reality, what appears to be the case is that they are faced with difficult dilemmas which are handled by working towards their own 'synthesis of Asian and British values'. Drury(1991) draws attention to the existence of two sets of socio-cultural systems in the lives of second-generation girls, which can be a valuable asset due to the ability to be used flexibly, allowing access to different cultural resources according to the context in which they find themselves. Probably the main reason why Naman did not report of any culture and/or identity conflicts due to the bicultural socialisation that he was experiencing was due to his gender and age. Perhaps the situation is not so distressing for Asian boys.

A general notion of Asian family life includes images of extended family, arranged marriages, and women's role in the family. Parent-child conflicts are likely to occur with regards to issues of individual freedom; gender based double standards; cultural identity and assimilation; dating and marriage; and social change (Kurian, 1986). In Britain the pattern of life for Asian families are undergoing constant change due to impact of the culture of the host community.

The notion of 'izzat' (honour/pride) is clearly a dominant feature of the Asian culture, however the importance attached as only applicable to girls and therefore reinforcing gender inequalities is highly questionable. The constraints of the culture and the limits of the extent to which girls can behave in an autonomous manner can have obvious disabling effects on the development of the 'self concept' (Ghuman, 1994). During adolescence and identity formation British Asians can experience role confusion in not being clear about their position being a minority in a host society in an attempt to reconcile the clashing values and norms of their family with that of the school. Alternatively, with the support of their peer group they may successfully synthesize the values of both cultures and develop a bicultural outlook/identity (Ghuman, 1994).

Although Asian doctors' families are very heterogeneous- they differ in terms of religion, cast, language and traditions - there are a number of common features of family life and their notions about culture. As already mentioned Asian families are fairly stable, with family break-up less common than many other groups in the UK (White and Woolet, 1992). The close family network aids a sense of belonging for Asian children and young people (Anwar, 1981; Stopes-Roe and Cockrane, 1990). However, it is important to note that we need to understand children's own reflection of their family life rather than generalising 'different' types of family situations. The cause of conflict between parents and young people within Asian communities is the existence of a 'generation gap' rather than cultural differences between Asian and white families (Anwar, 1981). 'Culture' itself is not a clearly defined homogeneity and there exists a problem for such views to be encouraged as they may clash with the beliefs of many families. It is therefore important to avoid cultural stereotypes to be applied to every member of the minority group.

Most of the children interviewed regarded their fathers as the head of the family and the chief decision maker which reflects the ideology of Asian families as being authoritarian and patriarchal in structure (Ghuman, 1994). In comparison, the mothers are given a subordinate and submissive position which is legitimised by claiming that it is 'part of the culture' (Drury, 1991). Anwar (1981) suggests that middle class parents are less conservative in outlook and less restrictive. This was clearly reflected in the interviews that I conducted with the doctors' children. Although Asian children are comfortable with their family, they expressed negative opinion about their schools and peers.

Discrimination

In white dominated schools children feel discriminated because of their colour.

> So many girls are having birthday parties. They are inviting everybody in the class, but not me, why is that? I invited all the girls from my class but only Jane asked me to her birthday, others didn't. Chloe told me several times that I am brown.
> (Registrar's daughter, age 7)

Not only the children talked about their own problems but also their parents felt strongly about their children's disappointment.

> There is indirect discrimination at school. My son secured highest marks in music to qualify for a scholarship. The music teacher and headmaster didn't recommend him for the scholarship. It is hidden discrimination. If it was a white boy they could have given the scholarship. That year the scholarship was not given to anybody. I guessed why they took this decision but did not challenge.
> (Registrar's wife, age 38)

> My son passed law exam and wanted to be a barrister. He could not get a place for training. As you know that these children are being discriminated due to their race. My son is very bright, he is frustrated. Now he works in a law firm. My other son is a brilliant boy. He did medicine in this country and worked as a registrar to become a cardiologist. The consultant in the cardiology department was a white man, who said: 'You better forget your ambition. If you want to be a consultant you may find it easier in psychiatry.' My son was heartbroken. He left the job and went to America after passing an exam. There he works as a cardiology specialist now.
> (Consultant's wife, age 58)

Parental pressure

Medical profession in some Asian countries have enjoyed a privileged position in the society and the overseas doctors practising in this country sometimes value medicine as the only option for their children. Anecdotal evidence suggests that they pressurise their children to study medicine in this country. This is illustrated in the following quote:

> My father is a medical consultant, he wants me to be a consultant when I grow up. He says I must study all the time and should not waste time by playing football. Being a doctor you may not become rich but you won't be poor. My mum also says the same thing that I should be a doctor and my younger brother should be a doctor as well. My parents don't smoke or drink. They never go to the pubs. They send me to a private school. I must work hard so that I can be a doctor (consultant) like my father.

(Consultant's son, age 15)

On the other hand some parents did not want their children to do medicine. A doctor's wife commented:

> My son did chartered accountancy and did MBA and now he is the Financial Director of an International company. So he has done very well. My daughter is a dentist. None of them wanted to go into medicine, they were clever enough but they found that their father's life was too demanding. They didn't want to do it.

(Consultant's wife, age 56)

Conclusions

The evidence presented in this chapter suggests that overseas doctors and their families indeed experience unique sources of stress related to their minority status. However, the evidence from the interview data supports some of our previous findings (Rout, 1989; Rout, 1996; Rout and Rout, 1993) that these doctors are often disadvantaged and have to cope with additional stressors linked to racial issues. Their wives and children also face enormous difficulties in coping with discrimination and isolation. Therefore, organisations should be aware of the need to relieve and eliminate some of the major stressors. There may be a need for the doctors and their spouses to understand the strategies they implement in dealing with stress related problems to which they are exposed and/or likely to be exposed. Also, there is a need for giving opportunity to ventilate feelings, discussing problems and discovering ways of solving problems. Children in Asian doctors' families need support and understanding from the parents rather than subjected to too much pressure for achieving. 'If children in Asian families living in Britain are to be comfortable about themselves in respect of their diverse experiences of culture, then it would seem important that they are encouraged to develop their identities without pressure' (Rout et al 1996).

5 Doctors' Spouses and Children

The previous chapters have already introduced some important issues related to doctors' spouses. This chapter will concentrate on non-medical spouses, housewives and doctors' children. These will include some literature survey and qualitative data from our interviews.

It is suggested by a number of writers (Cooke and Rousseau, 1984; Myerson, 1990; Billings and Moos, 1982) that wives' behaviour and attitudes are important factors in buffering or reducing the effect of stress on the family. For example, Burke and Belcourt, (1974) examined the compatibility of 190 husband-wife pairs (husbands with either accountants or engineers) and their impact on stress management. They found that the more compatible were the wives and husbands, the greater was the likelihood of coping with stress-related problems at work and at home. Doctors are not different from these occupational groups in relation to their family and social life.

In comparison with other professions doctors' marriages are often unsatisfactory even though they remain married (Vaillant et al 1974; Gerber, 1983; Garvey and Tuason, 1979). In a study of the marriages of a group of American doctors, it was found that 'lack of time for self, family and fun', was a major source of conflict perceived by both partners (Gabbard et al 1987). It was also found from the same study that the men blamed excessive hours spent at work, while their spouses complained of lack of intimacy. The doctors in this study accused their spouses of lack of sexual interest or sympathy for their job while their partners claimed that they did not talk to them adequately or render emotional support. The partners blamed each other for not making an effort to listen to each other.

Doctors' wives were four times more likely to commit suicide than other women (Sakinofsky, 1980). There is evidence from psychiatrists to show that doctors' wives do suffer from emotional stress (Nelson, 1978; Barker, 1980; Bennet, 1979). Miles and colleagues studied 20 physicians' wives who had been inpatients in British Columbia and found the following: 90% had a primary diagnosis of depression, 95% had personality disorders of hysterical and passive aggressive types, 90% had a history of suicidal ideation or attempts, and 54% had drug and/or alcohol problems (Miles et al 1975).

The causes of stress in the doctors' families have been analysed by several doctors' wives (Nelson, 1978; Horder, 1982; Gray, 1982; Rout, 1996), but these papers have been anecdotal and little empirical research appears to have been done in this area. Hence it was felt desirable to do an in-depth research, in order to isolate more precisely the specific stresses being experienced by doctors and their spouses. Identification of the sources of stress is a necessary first stage in improving the quality of life for doctors and their families. The aim of this investigation was therefore to extend our previous research on doctors' stress by examining the impact of these stresses on their families. Specifically, the study aimed to elucidate specific stressors and coping strategies of doctors and their spouses.

Doctors' wives' stress

When doctors' wives were asked "what element of your spouse's job causes unhappiness in your family life?" All the wives expressed their dissatisfaction about their husband's detachment from family and excessive commitment to work. One of the doctor's wives despondently expressed:

> Nowadays I hardly see my husband because he is working very hard. He is detached, indifferent and only loves work and money. There is no communication between us and there is no intimacy between us any more.

Couples working together are not immune to developing gaps in their relationship. One of the doctor's wives regrettably expressed:

> Our children have left home for University education. I decided to do some kind of job and luckily my husband who is a single handed doctor offered me his practice manager job which I accepted with delight thinking that we will be together most of the time and will feel closer to each other than before. Sadly the picture is different. He has joined a group of fund-holding GPs and keeps himself busy all the time. Now I find that whenever we are together he talks of nothing but fund-holding, patients, money and savings from allocated budget etc. We have no intimacy or social life. I regret accepting his offer of the job.

A supportive and sympathetic wife working together with her husband may not be able to maintain the close personal relationship. One disheartened wife spoke:

> We had a brilliant life when my husband was in the army. Things have changed since he got this single handed practice. I found him extremely busy and then I decided to become his practice manager. I find that I have changed myself. We are eating either fast junk food or frozen food as I can never find any time for cooking meals at home. I think we are no longer marital partners but business colleagues. Our sex life is almost non existent. We are seriously thinking of immigrating to America.

A major theme running through the interviews was that of communication problem. One of the doctor's wives was seriously concerned about her husband's long hours of absence from home. She felt helpless because she believed that her husband was not open to her. In despair she said:

> My husband is always busy with his job, well.... that's what he says that his job has become more demanding due to the recent changes in the NHS. I am beginning to doubt his claims. I wonder whether he is involved in any extra marital affair. He shows no emotional attachment towards me and we have non of those warm personal relationship now. I think our marriage is on the brink. I don't know what to do? I feel totally lost.

> We are unable to solve little problems at home as we have no patience to listen to each other. I feel a barrier has developed between us causing difficulty in communication and this barrier I am sure is his work pressure.

Exploring time factor in-depth, researchers suggest that spouses feel a strong need for time to talk with each other, while male doctors are more likely to use their leisure periods participating in sports amenities, on home improvement projects, or catching up on professional reading (Ziegler, 1992). In this case discrepancies in communication style could be considered as one of the important factors for consideration.

Both doctors may bring their self-defeating personality traits to the marriage as well as lack of experience in how to build a balanced family life (Zeigler, 1992). Without conscious effort the couple may find their problems remain unresolved and the consequence on the family is paramount. In many cases they do not like to talk about the problems as this may cause situations to worsen. Over time the family playing by this and other stress enhancing rules will develop a deep seated, festering abscess of anger, hurt and fear which poisons intimacy and trust in the relationship (Zeigler, 1991). The couples may drift farther and farther; as a result they may look outside for warmth and love and may have extra marital affairs.

Many wives felt that their husbands' work patterns have changed following the NHS reforms in the 1990s. They are having to work harder and keeping away from their families. They were sympathetic but showed resentment. The following comments are self explanatory:

> After the recent changes he works late in the surgery and brings paper work home.
>
> He is physically and psychologically exhausted and gets irritated for very little things.
>
> Nowadays he spends time away from home for Post Graduate meetings and I am stuck at home with the children.

Doctors' professional wives

Professional work does not stay within the boundary of 9-5 o'clock and 5 days week schedule. This spills over to evenings and weekends due to emergencies, meetings, conferences, keeping up with the literature and preparing articles for professional and academic journals. The more ambitious the spouses are the more they are committed to work. When they have young children at home the problem escalates. We have interviewed a couple where husband was a general practitioner and wife was an academic. They had conflict over looking after children and dividing the household responsibilities. For example the doctor's wife said:

> When I said to my husband I have a conference to attend to next weekend and you have to look after the children. You have to take them to dance school, music teacher, swimming and stagecoach. I cannot do these next week. My husband said, 'I would like to do that but I am on-call. Who will look after them when I am out for visiting patients?' Then I said, 'I don't know anything. Whenever it comes to my job there is a problem. I do not understand your commitment to your practice. You are in a partnership you could arrange that!' He said 'I can't but I will leave the children in Michael's house'. I said, 'I do not like my children to be treated like bags of potatoes left somewhere like that. I shall not go to the conference. At the end I had to sacrifice. Why is that? This always happens. I am furious about this. I do not like this type of arrangement. We have no understanding and no communication. I just carry on. We don't get on. I just do it for my children. I don't have any sympathy for him. He never supports me when I need it.
>
> (Lecturer, age 37)

The end product of this is a considerable loss for the marriage by the couple not getting on so well. This couple didn't have any support for each other when they needed it most. This view was also voiced by another doctor's professional wife:

> I do not need anybody's support now. When I was in a traumatic condition he never supported me, physically or mentally.
>
> (Lecturer, age 35)

Another doctor's wife who was in a professional job felt that her doctor husband is inconsiderate to her career and always gives priority to his own job.

She complained:

> I have a full-time job. We share the responsibility of dropping children at school in the morning but he always has an excuse to escape and dump the responsibility on me as if I have no obligation to my job. He has this divine weapon 'responsibility to his patients' that he uses against any logical argument and wins. But what about the responsibility to his wife and children? My husband always puts his work first. I think doctor husbands are a hindrance to their wives careers.
>
> (Senior lecturer, age 33)

Another doctor's wife mentioned about her unhappiness regarding managing the home.

> I do the cooking, arrange birthday parties, dinner parties, holiday arrangements and other social arrangements. My husband always says he shares these with me but only when he is asked to do something, he does it. Now I put forward my views quite frankly we should do 50 : 50.
>
> (Teacher, age 35)

On the other hand some doctors' wives were happy about their arrangements at home. For example:

> My friends always tell me that we are not very conventional couple because we share the housework and childcare proportionally. I tell them if we don't do this we cannot face up to the reality of the modern world.
>
> (Company Manager, age 35)

Meera came to England with her husband after her marriage and immediately she had a child to look after. She could not pursue a career which she had dreamed of. She was in a dilemma - whether to start her career when the baby was very young or leave it a little longer. She knew that her husband was traditionally raised and expected that he would hang on to the notion of woman's child rearing role. One evening she asked her husband if she could go to the nearest university to do a degree. Her husband was pleased to see Meera's interest in studies. He took over, willingly, many of their home responsibilities. They had very little money to spare for luxury because her husband was only a junior doctor. But they were happy. She said:

> It was rather very hard to bring up the child and doing the degree at the same time. The money was tight. We could not afford to go out as often as we wanted to, but we had an excellent child minder. Then he started going to nursery. My husband helped me a lot in looking after Miresh (name of their son) and giving me moral support. I finished the degree when my son was going to school. He is a lovely child. I achieved what I wanted. I am very happy about that.
>
> (Lecturer, age 25)

When we interviewed the doctor husband, he said:

> I am very proud of my wife's achievement. I am a good father to my son. I learnt cooking now. I help her in many things what I didn't do before. I feel that I am very modern and 90's man. I have a full life.
>
> (SHO, age 28)

This is a rare case in the interview sample. Now more and more bright young women want to pursue a career. They need more support from their spouses and from their employers.

Telephone interruption was a major source of irritation for many doctors' families. A young doctor's wife remarked:

> The main thing that irritates me is the constant interruption of our family life by telephone. It is so regular that sometimes I wonder, how do the patients know the precise minute we start our family dinner? I sometimes joke that if you are not sure whether your telephone is working or not, just start the dinner. I can guarantee that the telephone will ring.
>
> (Accountant, age 30)

There is enormous pressure for a doctor to get the job done and not to show any emotional reaction. This may make a doctor detached from the rest of the world including the family members. For example one doctor's wife in our interview sample expressed the problem in her family:

> My husband does not like to talk about any problem at all. When I talk about my problems he doesn't listen to me. He is a detached person. He has no emotion. When I cry he doesn't bother to know the reason. Even when my parents died he never put his hand on my shoulder to console me. I sometimes do not understand his personality. What he is made up of. It sounds strange after 15 years of marriage. You just try to carry on.
>
> (Practice Manager, age 36)

Another doctor's wife felt lonely and isolated when she gave birth to her first child in the hospital. She narrated:

> I was heavily pregnant with my first baby. He knew that I have to go to the hospital within a few days. When I told him that I am getting some kind of pain he ignored me. He said 'go back to sleep it may be false alarm'. He was tired after the on-call duty, he wanted to have rest. I asked him again to wake up and take me to the hospital. He didn't respond. I was in agony and severe pain. I was ignorant as to what to do. Then I shouted and cried. He got up in the end and took me to the hospital and left me there. I had to stay in the labour room for 24 hours. He never came to see me... saying that he was on-call and tired. I had my first baby without my husband with me. I was young and naive. I resented the fact that I shouldn't have married to a doctor. He explained to me afterwards although I am still not convinced. I never wanted another child until now. I do not want to go through the trauma again.
>
> (Teacher, age 24)

The problem doesn't stop after having a baby. She went on to say:

> For me it was rather very difficult time. I was on my own all the time. My husband was working long hours. At night when the baby was crying I had to feed him in the other bedroom as I was breast-feeding. I didn't want to disturb my husband's sleep. I had to cope on my own. I never got any support.
>
> (Teacher, age 24)

Another theme running through the interviews was that of emotional detachment as a doctor's wife expressed:

> My doctor husband is like a solid rock. He does not talk about anything at all. He does not show any emotion. When I have a problem I like to express myself. When I talk about this he never listens to me. I become noisy some days. He doesn't care - he says, 'Perhaps it is your pre-menstrual tension.' This makes me very angry. I just keep it to myself and sometimes cry.
>
> (Manager of a retail store, age 31)

This suppression of emotion may be harmful in the long run. Women living like this may develop any form of psychological disorder.

Some wives complained that their doctor husbands were selfish, unsociable and workaholics. I interviewed Mrs Kar. After several requests she finally agreed to be interviewed. I knew her through friends. She seemed to be a nice person, but she claimed that she was extremely busy for last few months due to her husband's commitment to work. Hence could not talk to me earlier. She told me:

> My husband is selfish and always busy in his work. He does not bother to socialise with my friends and other people around us. I am very angry with him at times. Sometimes I am very short-tempered. When he does not respond to me, I throw him a slap and run outside. He is a battered husband (laugh). He gets into my nerves some days. Then I calm down. I realise my fault and then get on with life. He does not look after the children. He does not know who I invite and how many times I contact his parents, my parents and my relations. He is totally immersed in his work. I work in an office. I do not work erratic hours. If I do not work I will be mad in this house by just looking after the children and the house.
>
> (Social worker, age 39)

First I could not work out the term 'battered husband'. As the conversation progressed I came to know that her husband was an excellent consultant but poor family man. She learnt to cope with him by making noise and slapping him at times. Also she said:

> His outlook is good. I work outside and go out with my friends whenever I like. I come home late. It is fine with him. He does not mind. But when he comes home late in the evenings I attack

him. We don't like argument to continue. We compromise this way.

This is a classic case. I wonder how they lived together for so many years (they have been married for 15 years). The husband is dominated, controlled and treated unfairly by the wife. What are the effects on their children! This consultant may come from a unhappy family where the mother argues a lot and beats the father. The father may have poor self-esteem and lack assertiveness in the marriage. The son may not be clear on what is considered normative behaviour in marriages. He may have anxiety about separation and loneliness. The doctor's wife also had told me that they came from different backgrounds.

Mr Simon Bate is an excellent surgeon who earned his fame quite early in his career. He is praised both by patients and his colleagues alike. He was happily married with two children. All was well until the children left home for university education. Mr Bate spent more and more time in hospital and less time with his wife. He always had an excuse for his wife. "I had a really difficult case to operate which took seven hours". His wife suspected that there was something wrong. She said:

> I thought that once the children left home our relationship would become stronger and more pleasant. Simon's behaviour changed quite suddenly. He mentioned a few times that he is missing the children. I noticed that he spent less and less time at home. I had the feeling that he was in a hurry to get out of the house. He would say that he had to review private patients or a colleague is requesting to give him a hand for an emergency case. I was too naive to understand any complicacy or foul play. One afternoon, his colleague's wife (a good friend of mine) telephoned me for a social chat. During the conversation she asked me if everything was okay between us. I was surprised at this and asked her if she knew something that I did not. She was unwilling to have any further discussion on that topic but I raised the subject a few minutes later. I was 'gob-smacked' when she told me that she had seen Simon and Rachel (the theatre sister) together on several occasions outside the hospital. I felt as if lightening had struck on my head. A few weeks later I was admitted to hospital with an abdominal swelling and was diagnosed to have ovarian cancer.

> Simon came to see me everyday, but I felt we were miles apart. There has been no change in the situation since after I came home from the hospital. I felt so weak that I had no strength to raise the topic of his adultery. There is little point in discussing this while my days are numbered.
>
> (Nurse, age 46)

One would expect the wife would get tender loving medical care from a doctor husband, but this does not happen in this case.

> When I became pregnant with my first child he used to ignore my symptoms. One day I was sick several times. Without comforting me he said 'This is quite natural for a mother-to-be'. I started complaining afterwards, but he ignored me. I learnt to live with it now. Most of the time I treat myself by taking paracetamols without knowing the exact treatment for the pain.
>
> (Researcher, age 27)

Sexual involvement with patients is an important area which is very rarely mentioned in the literature. An excellent book by Myers (1994) is an exception. There are several cases published in medical newsletters. Not only do these doctors shake their marital equilibrium by having relationship with patients but also this is unethical. In addition to the marital crisis they face enormous humiliation from the public. The wives and family members of these doctors had to contain with feelings of shame. A typical case of this category is as follows:

Dr Simpson was reported to the General Medical Council for professional misconduct. This was also reported to the police as indecent assault. When the details came out it was revealed that Dr Simpson had had sexual relationship with a patient. When the matter became public he realised that he will not be able to defend himself and therefore immediately resigned from the job and from the GMC. However, this created a deep wound for his wife. She commented:

> I am shocked and anybody in my situation would divorce her husband. I am living with him because my children are young. I am still confused what to do.
>
> (GP's wife, age 46)

Doctors' children

There is no literature available on doctors' children in this country. Most of the published data on doctors' children are exclusively American, which emphasised the negative aspects. However, we conducted a qualitative study during 1995 and 1996 and found that doctors' children are subjected to high expectations from family members - especially parents.

Doctors not only want achievement for themselves but also they pressurise their children to achieve their full potential. A teenage daughter confronts her mother on many occasions.

> When I needed her she was not there for me. She had no time for me. She just pressurised me to study hard, do this do that but nothing else.
>
> (Girl, age 15)

Another teenager felt pressurised due to the parental conflict.

> "My father would not move an inch. They fight so much. I always try to keep them together. They don't talk to each other for months. When he is ready, resumes relations as if nothing has happened. The pressure is on me to study".
>
> (Boy, age 16)

Work pressure may not only dilute attention to the children but may make them feel neglected. A young mother with school going children resentfully said:

> We wait for him to come home on time to have evening meal with us but almost invariably get a telephone call saying 'darling I have a lot of things to ort out and I shall not be able to join you for dinner'........Sometimes if we are lucky to have dinner together, it is not uncommon for the telephone to ring as soon as he starts his meal and re-joins after we all finish ours......... ... My husband used to check children's home work but nowadays he never gets time to do so.
>
> (Doctor's wife, age 22)

All the children interviewed expressed their dissatisfaction about their fathers' heavy commitment to work and lack of time to play with them.

> My dad works very hard. He does not have time to play with me. I always ask him why he is late. He says he has to see patients. When I talk to him he does not pay any attention to me. He does not smile, he does not talk. It makes me unhappy. Sometimes when he arrives at home the phone rings. Then it is my bedtime.
> (Girl, age 9)

This view was also voiced by another doctor's daughter.

> My dad comes home late and he is grumpy all the time. He does not listen to me probably he does not think it is important. I don't try to talk to him so much now. I would like him to come home early, so that we could have dinner together.
> (Girl, age 11)

In a dual doctor's marriage both parents may display workaholic attitude which can harm the relationship between parents and children. Two doctors' marriage is different than any dual-career marriage because medical professionals' activities are reinforced by personal expectations and those of society (Taylor et al 1987). Research shows that in many of the dual career families the female professional takes most responsibility for home management and childcare with her own career demands (Fine, 1981). Due to the demands of professional commitment, doctor mother has less hours to be with her children than housewives. The children might feel neglected for not getting enough attention and care from the mother.

This is not always the case.

> My mum is a doctor. She not only looks after me but also takes care of her patients. She gets lot of money. I buy lot of good things with it. I am very happy that my mum and dad both are doctors.
> (Girl, age 11)

Illness in doctor's family

Chronic illness affects family members emotionally and behaviourally. There are several examples in our interview sample on the problems in doctors families especially when there is illness in the family. These are special kind of problems which pressurise the marriage and family life. Dr Worsley's wife had been suffering from rheumatoid arthritis for four years. She was taking drugs regularly and her life style was changed dramatically after the diagnosis of rheumatoid arthritis. She was teaching full time in a university which she reduced to half-time and she had to give up her hobbies requiring physical exercise. Although she was enjoying her job she was frustrated at times because of her severity of arthritis. She told us that her husband is very apathetic to the whole situation and does not give any attention to her sickness. They did not do anything together any more. She told us sarcastically, "we even don't argue any more, which we did nearly every day". She felt that due to her arthritis her husband was detached and didn't want to know her any more. They used to eat out at least once a week and went to the cinema regularly. They took the children for swimming twice a week and entertained friends and families. Due to her illness they have stopped everything. They don't have any intimate relationship. She no longer felt attractive to her husband and felt rejected. She said:

> I feel rejected by everybody especially my husband. He was so good to me and always interested in me. Now he doesn't look at me. He is very quiet. He is not attracted towards me any more. Oh God..... why me? I haven't done anything drastically wrong in this life.
>
> (University lecturer, age 37)

Another classic example drawn from a conversation between two doctors' wives in a seminar. They both were complaining about their husbands' negligence when they were ill. Rachael told us that she had a major operation (hysterectomy) a year ago. Her husband never had any sympathy towards her. She was suffering from terrible pain after the operation. Her husband didn't take any time off for her. During the second week after her operation, she was having a bath, and when she had finished she could not get out of the bath. There was no one else in the house to help her. Her husband was at work and the children were at school. She said:

> I was in the bath for four hours until my husband came at lunch time. I was unable to ring because I was not able to get out of the bath. When he came for lunch he helped me to come out of the bath. Until then I was crying in the bath. I cannot forget the pain and agony I was going through. Men don't understand this.
>
> (Nurse, age 35)

Chloe said:

> David (her husband's name) looks extremely caring in front of other people, because he is polite and very soft spoken gentleman. When it comes to caring wife he is just opposite. When I had an operation he didn't want to know how I was feeling. He left my two children with me and went abroad to attend a conference for a week. I was struggling to get up from bed. He gave me a very sweet talk that he booked the ticket already. When I complained he told me that he wanted to get away from the dull and boring atmosphere at home. He was glad that he could avoid the home that week. I was very angry and disappointed with his attitude. I could not accept this type of attitude towards me at that time. I adjusted that due to my children. When I think of that situation I cannot forgive him. Even now he says he wants me to be strong and capable of managing everything even when I am ill. He wants me to maintain my look especially figure, run the house, look after the children etc. It is ridiculous. When he is ill he does not want to bother anybody. He takes his own temperature, BP, looks at his throat and takes his medicine. He just keeps everything within himself. Perhaps he expects me to be like that. I cannot be like that. He fails to realise that we are two different people with two different personalities.
>
> (Lecturer, age 32)

This view was also voiced by another doctor's wife who was a teacher.

> I had a terrible headache before going to school. I asked him to check my body temperature. Without looking at me he said, 'You

> don't have anything - you go to work'. I did go to work. After one lesson my body was shivering. I could not carry on. I had to leave the classroom and went straight to the staff common room and collapsed. One of my colleagues said, 'your husband is a doctor, didn't he check you before you came?' I didn't say anything to her. I was furious. I was muttering to myself. I asked him (husband) to look at my throat if I was developing anything. He ignored me. Over the years I have learnt to treat my own ailments.
>
> (Teacher, age 30)

When a doctor is ill himself (especially male) he handles it in a totally different manner.

Dr. Pandu had a bypass three months prior to our interview. His wife was concerned about his food habit and excess weight. Before the bypass he was taking very rich food prepared in oil and sugar but now his wife restricts oil and sugar in food preparation. Dr Pandu was not happy about that and was not eating properly. He was complaining about boiled food and bland diet. One day he was angry and frustrated during his dinner time, he left the dinner table without touching the food. His wife was very upset with Dr Pandu's behaviour and she narrated the event to me:

> My husband does not want the food I cook. After his bypass I have to be careful what I cook and how I cook. I do not use a lot of oil and sugar in my cooking. He doesn't like it. I do understand the difficulty. One day he was furious and shouted at me and never ate anything. I was heart broken and sulking.
>
> (Doctor's wife, age 40)

This type of behaviour could make life extremely hard. Dr Pandu's wife's intention was very clear: she wanted her husband to follow a diet according to the doctor's advice, but Dr Pandu did not appreciate that, instead he was very angry and hostile.

Illness in doctors' children

Doctors not only distance themselves from their wives when they are ill, but also they do the same when their children become ill. Doctors' wives take the sole responsibility for their sick children by taking them to their general practitioners and specialists. For example:

Dr Ali's daughter was ill due to an unknown viral infection, with a very high temperature and an unusual rash. Dr Ali's wife took her to hospital to a specialist who could not arrive at a conclusive diagnosis. She was very worried about her. She needed moral support from Dr Ali at that time, instead Dr Ali was preoccupied with his work schedule and the next day he had to fly to Paris to attend a conference. Although he rang home to find out about the child's health, Mrs Ali was not pleased about his decision to go to Paris without considering their daughter's illness.

> My husband does not bother about me or the children. He thinks that his work is his only duty.

This shows that doctors are too much dedicated to their work and pay little attention to their families.

Another example from a chronically ill child's parents is given below. In this case the father was a consultant physician and the mother was a housewife. Their son had cystic fibrosis, who needed the attention of parents. The doctor father was always busy in the hospital and in his private practice and the mother had to look after their son 24 hours a day throughout the year. She never had any outside help. At times she couldn't cope. She stayed at home most of the time and never had any outside life. The following example illustrates this:

> You see I don't have a minute for myself. I am always looking after Aman. My husband is never there to help me. He is always out in helping others.

Conclusions

Clearly, the material presented in this chapter illustrates that doctors' wives were indeed under pressure due to several factors. The main factors causing stress were: communications problem, concerns regarding their husbands excessive commitment to work, their husbands' detachment from the family and interruptions (Rout, 1996). The wives claimed that medicine was their husbands' first priority and they should understand that. Due to professional socialisation the doctor puts medicine as first priority before his wife and children (Myers, 1994). It was found that doctors' children and wives were neglected during their illness and doctors treated themselves when they were ill. This is of some concern for some doctors. Ideally, a study using both subjective and objective data is needed to determine the ongoing nature of these findings.

6 Managing Stress

In the previous chapters pressure and problem areas were divided according to different groups of doctors i.e. medical students, House Officers, Senior House Officers, consultants, general practitioners, women doctors, overseas doctors and their spouses, and doctors' spouses and children. This concluding chapter provides some suggestions for the problems cited in previous chapters and outlines some of the individual and organisational stress management strategies. There is no simple solution to these specific problems but the information may provide an adequate understanding of stress in doctors and their families. The solutions recommended may be considered as pointers.

Recognising stress

One of the first steps in dealing with stress is awareness of the problem. The doctor must carefully examine his or her stress in terms of professional and family demands. Depending on the problem steps must be taken to reduce the stress. Appropriate stress management strategies should be developed targeted at medical students, hospital doctors, general practitioners, and their family members to reduce or eliminate stress. Stress not only affect doctors' own health but it also may adversely affect patient care. Therefore there is a need for organisations, representing these doctors, to take appropriate action for reducing and managing stress. For example, the NHS and Family Health Services Authorities could take the initiative in consultation with those working in primary and secondary care to design and implement appropriate stress management strategies.

How can doctors' families survive

As mentioned already, recognising the problem is the first step to a solution. Secondly, it has to be accepted that doctors are human and therefore like any other people they are vulnerable to stress. This is not as simple as it sounds. In a couple's relationship, if one partner perceives the problem and other does not then communication breaks down.

How a problem is raised is also important. If problems are expressed in accusatory way the situation becomes argumentative. Myers (1994) gave some examples of reporting feelings which work better (e.g. 'we don't seem to talk as easily any more' or 'I feel unhappy that we can't talk like as we use to' as opposed to 'you never talk to me any more').

As mentioned in the previous chapter a child can feel the unhappiness between the parents from their arguments with each other without resolution. Therefore it is the responsibility of parents to resolve the problem/s without involving the child and find ways of not arguing in front of the child. If the problem is too serious outside help is needed. Also it is equally dangerous when both parents withdraw physically and emotionally from each other. For example, they do not do anything together, do not discuss anything, don't go out, socialise with other people and they don't have common friends.

The family is a major source of support for the individual, providing problem solving, listening, and accepting behaviour that is essential to alleviate stress, even though they may be unable to change the circumstances that created them. Myers et al (1975) found that people who were more integrated in society (i.e. being married with children and of higher socio-economic status) coped better with different negative life crises than those not as integrated. Support is also known to have beneficial effect in preventing medical complications. It was found in a study by Sosa et al (1980) in Guatemala, that expectant mothers accompanied by friends had fewer complications than those who were unaccompanied.

As mentioned earlier wives' behaviour and attitudes are important factors in bettering or reducing the effect of stress on the family (Cooke and Rousseau, 1984; Billings and Moos, 1982). Therefore, it is necessary for the partners to try to understand the problem and support each other in the home environment in order to overcome the factors contributing to stress. Satisfaction in marriage was related to the time a couple spent talking to each other (Hall, 1988). Regular outing to a cinema or eating out as a couple, is important. This time together is very useful to resume the relationship without interruptions.

Before taking any hasty decision about the relationship the doctor and the spouse should consult a well trained and experienced professional who can advise and assist with treatment. For example, the doctor and the spouse should first consult their general practitioner. This will uncover some of the problems that the doctor and the spouse are facing. Then a referral can be made by the general practitioner to an appropriate professional i.e. counsellor or clinical psychologist.

Dr Ray and Mrs Ray had been married for ten years. They had two daughters. Both were working in the same practice as general practitioners. They had been separated for five months when we interviewed them. Mrs Ray told us the separation was temporary and she would like to go back to him. Children were very unhappy and this reflected in their school work and behaviour. Mrs Ray was feeling guilty because she initiated the separation without thinking of the consequences on the children and on her own mental health. She said:

> There was lot of argument and fighting in front of children. We could not stop the tension between us. We could not talk to each other. I thought this is not the way a couple should live. Therefore I initiated the separation. Now I am confused and feeling guilty about the whole thing. I don't know what to do.

The decision to separate has been made quickly because of Mrs Ray's pressure. Although this was taken jointly it was very ambiguous. The couple need counselling or/and clinical psychologist or/and marital therapy because it seems that they had a lot of unresolved conflicts between them. A trained counsellor and/or marital therapist would help the couple to think through their problems clearly. There are empirical evidences that therapy works well to help couples (Jacobson, 1978). Some doctors may not like to see professionals in their own area of living because they don't trust them or they know them personally. It is important to recognise this problem and these doctors could seek professional help from outside their area of living.

Some of the case studies cited in previous chapters showed some symptoms of stress i.e. anxiety, sleeplessness, anger, headache and unhappiness. Behavioural factors included alcohol consumption, drug usage and smoking. Doctors and spouses must notice these symptoms or similar changes in his/her partner.

There are certain specialities, which are so labour intensive that they affect the family more. For example, we have mentioned a quote from a surgeon who found it very stressful when he was continuously on his feet in the operating theatre. In these cases wives need to be supportive and understanding. They should understand the work pattern of their husbands.

Doctor's wife

In our interview sample we found that some doctors' non-working wives felt lonely and isolated. Try to find a job even if you get less money. You may have to forget that you were born with a silver spoon in your mouth. You have to think of the situation now. You could learn something new in an evening course in a local college. This will widen your world. You could go to the local library and read newspapers, classics and other kind of novels and best sellers to enhance your learning, understanding and education.

One doctor's wife mentioned that she was thinking of joining a course but this never happened even though she was on her own after her children went to university. They should take action immediately. These women need support from their husbands and also from local support groups. We arranged a local support group for doctors and their wives for meeting once in a month to talk about problems. It was short-lived. We do not know the reason behind it. However, we could not keep up with the group due to our heavy commitment. We are planning again to contact the doctors and their spouses to resume the support group.

Married women doctors with children find it difficult to meet the demands of many roles. These demands include their roles as doctors, wives, mothers and home-makers. When they cannot meet these obligations as they would like to they may feel under stress. Married women doctors who try to do too much by themselves, who do not delegate jobs, and whose husbands are not helping are main subjects for role strain. This might lead to marital difficulty when it becomes unbearable. Some suggestions are given for dual career couples and working women elsewhere in this chapter which is appropriate for married women doctors.

Overseas doctors and spouses

From our study it was found that many overseas doctors and their spouses do not have any close family or friends to turn to for help. They should recognise the need for outside help. They need to make a conscious effort to have good friends to avoid loneliness. This can be extremely beneficial and rewarding and might help to counteract stress. Friends can provide moral support, practical advice and happiness. Talking through a problem will help the doctors and their spouses see things clearly.

Overseas doctors and their spouses might find it difficult to seek outside help due to their cultural, racial, ethnic and religious backgrounds. This might influence the therapist. There is a scarcity of therapists with non-white backgrounds. It may be easier to seek help from a therapist who has similar background with shared beliefs and values so that he/she can understand the problem clearly. On the other hand if the therapist comes from the same background and has contacts with the community this problem is different. Question of confidentiality and privacy may arise. It may be difficult in finding a therapist if couples have different backgrounds (e.g. mixed marriages).

Having your own general practitioner

Many couples turn to their general practitioner for common marital problems but with some vague complaint of unhappiness. Myers, in his excellent paper, described common marital problems that couples bring to their family, physicians' methods of assessment, and treatment guidelines (Myers, 1984).

It is not uncommon for some doctors to find themselves caught in the middle of other professional colleagues' marital problems especially when they are registered as patients in his/her surgery. Sometimes it is difficult to be honest and open because of his/her relationship with the couple as a professional colleague, a friend and as a patient. A typical case is worth noting. When we interviewed a general practitioner he said:

> Both Dr and Mrs Crossly are registered in my practice but they are also my family friends. They rarely come to the surgery with medical problems but recently both have been to see me on several occasions but separately. I have heard accusations from each side how the other been unfaithful and doing things behind back. I have tried to help them as their general practitioner and also family friend. They have been separated for six months. Dr Crossly has lost great amount of weight with other clinical symptoms which has really worried me. I have already referred him to a specialist colleague. Mrs Crossly rang me to enquire about him stating that she has been told by him that he is a terminal case. This put me in a very difficult situation. I was unable to give any information due to confidentiality. This is not an unusual situation but when the patient is a professional colleague and a close friend it becomes difficult to deal with as you can't take side, although, you want to help them.
>
> (GP, age 41)

Even though general practitioners do not provide family therapy they refer their patients to a trained therapist. However, some doctors do not go to their general practitioners and instead they go directly to a specialist or ask their general practitioner for a referral. Some doctors even do not have their own general practitioner. The worst scenario is some of the doctors go to their general practitioner with marital problems they are not assessed thoroughly, they are eventually referred to specialists. For example:

> Mrs Patel went to see her general practitioner about her marital problem. She complained that she was depressed and could not sleep at night. The couple were arguing frequently over every little thing. She was desperate to get some help. The general practitioner took only 5 minutes to listen to her and prescribed a tranquilliser. He advised her to wait until she gets the letter of invitation from the local hospital to see a clinical psychologist. She received a letter of invitation after six weeks. This didn't help her to solve her problem.

Some doctors are very private individuals. They do not like to talk about their personal problems to anyone even to their spouses. Typical example:

> My husband does not like to discuss about any problems to anyone including me. I know him now perfectly. Therefore I don't even bother to ask him.
>
> (GP, age 33)

This may be due to personality or traits that run in the family. There may be some past experience (mistrust of others or no one is interested in their conversations) for which the individual does not want to communicate. Some people rely on themselves. For example a doctor's wife solved her own problem on many occasions without getting any outside help. She explained:

> I had to struggle many a time for different problems. Most of the time solved them successfully but occasionally I had to go through a lot of stress. It took a long time to learn to be self-reliant by using different coping strategies: determination, meditation, working harder, focusing on the problem, thinking of previous problem solving skills and learning from friends who solved similar problems before. I do not like to talk about my home and marital problems to anybody.
>
> (Registrar's wife, age 39)

However, this self-reliance, based on individualism may not work for the couple when they are in marital stress. Shared communication is required for marital stress. The socialisation in medical school rewards self-reliance and denials of existence of any problem. The medical ethics is to work hard for others. For example:

> I don't get any stress. I have no problem. Well I have some problem but I can solve them. I can see the problems at work before hand then I try to solve them. Even if I cannot I don't get stress. For example: there was always shortages in the NHS. This is not new. Why should I get stress if money is not allocated for certain operations. I have to adjust with limited resources.
>
> (Consultant surgeon, age 50)

Suggestions to specific problems at the workplace

Developing social and managerial skills

According to Davidson (1978) you must find out the reason of disliking the job and then possibly you could delegate the job to someone else, or you could break the job into smaller units so that it may be easier to finish. Paperwork was one of the top five stressors for general practitioners (Rout and Rout, 1993) and hospital doctors (Rout and Rout, 1999). We noticed that general practitioners were accumulating paperwork but were not dealing with it. They could break the paperwork into smaller units and distribute evenly for the week and do a little everyday rather than piling up and finding no time for it. It is often recommended to handle each piece of paper only once and it is worth acquiring the habit. You can sort your papers daily according to priority (low, medium and high priority). Then you could concentrate first on the high priority pile of paper. You may not feel pressurized if you don't get time to handle the low priority paperwork. This principle of selection applies to other reading materials. For example, if you want to keep up with important developments in the professional field, you could read summary or review journals. Then you could choose articles or books which contain detail information for developing your skills.

The stress caused by patients' expectation, job demand, interruption and administration entail social and managerial skill, which can be developed by training. Considerations may be given to providing doctors and other health care professionals with more time management, people management and work organisation skill development, as this might well help them to overcome some of the stressors of their job. These skills might also help them in trying to minimise the impact of their job on their family life by providing them with more quality time at home. Patients' expectations have increased many times over, and for some their 'wants' are more than their 'needs'. It is quite possible that the patients' charter may have empowered patients excessively to the detriment of the doctor-patient relationship. The expectations of the patients could be made more realistic by increasing their understanding through discussion between doctors and patients. The patient participation group movement has been in existence for several years in some areas of England and is perceived as important (Agas et al 1991); other branches need to be encouraged and helped.

Interruptions

Interruption of any kind is one of the major factors of stress in general practice (Rout and Rout, 1993). Perhaps it is more damaging when working in a complex task, where larger chunks of time are required for the flow of thought. Dealing with interruptions can be a problem for any health care professional. Rutherford (1978) suggested that every time you respond to drop-ins with a pleasant chat you give a silent licence by encouraging them to interrupt again. This can be prevented by telling the interrupter that you are in the middle of some important project which needs to be finished. You give another time to the interrupter for a meeting. If the behaviour of the interrupter continues, you could ignore him/her until he/she gets the message. For interruption you can make a time log to get some idea of the size of the interruption. You could identify the people or events who are responsible for the interruptions and find solutions to correct the situations.

Learning to say no

Some doctors find it hard to refuse other people's request for jobs to be done. This causes stress because they lack assertion skills. Therefore you must learn to say no, with firmness. If you find it difficult to say no, you could examine the reasons. Is it due to lack of assertiveness, or is it due to not knowing your own capabilities? In these circumstances you could consider to take an assertiveness training course.

Stress management programmes

Today, stress management programmes are increasingly popular. It is believed that stress management can reduce stress and its effects by using a technique or combination of techniques. Stress management techniques are generally divided into three categories:

1 Alterations of environment and/or life style (time management, proper nutrition, stopping smoking, drinking, exercise etc.).

2 Alterations of personality and/or perception (assertiveness training, refuting irrational beliefs, Type A behaviour modification, etc.).

3 Alterations of biological responses (progressive relaxation, meditation, biofeedback, autogenics etc.).
(Monat and Lazarus, 1991)

These divisions are somewhat arbitrary. It is important to note that some of the techniques can be placed under more than one categories above (e.g. exercise can be placed under the category of biological responses). De Frank and Cooper (1987) classify stress management programmes into two levels of intervention i.e. at the individual level, and at the group or organizational level. Sometimes a combination of programmes is offered in organisations.

Health promotion programmes

Health promotion and stress prevention schemes are labelled as: 'wellness programmes', 'treatment of chemically dependent employees', 'employee assistant programmes', 'lifestyle change programmes' and the like (Cooper, 1982). In recent years, there has been an increase in employee health programmes in the USA, in order to reduce the escalating cost of employee health care insurance and litigation. Today, in the UK, this trend is spreading slowly.

An Employee Assistant Programme (EAP) provides a number of services for the employees to adjust to the work environment. These programmes include stress management classes, personal counselling and classes on coping (Ivancevich et al 1990), career change counselling, job retraining, and support for families of stressed employees. In other cases a professional person is employed by the organisation to assist the employees. Some other organisations are developing several services to preserve the enthusiasm of employees - for example health gyms, spas, exercise and child-care services.

An example of the wellness programme is the 'Staywell' programme, introduced by 'Control Data Corporation'. The programme includes specific high risk areas such as smoking, fitness, nutrition and weight control, hypertension and stress. Specific activities to change life-style and improve health were planned for each employee. In addition, a follow-up programme was introduced where the employees formed groups where the members of the group helped each other to sustain the change in their behaviour. The outcome of the wellness programme is most impressive. The outcomes included 50% reductions in sickness rates and absenteeism, increases in job performance, improved attitude towards work, improved stamina and loss of weight (Hall and Goodale, 1986).

One of the most popular methods in dealing with stress is physical fitness (Rosch and Pelletier, 1987). Pepsico Inc. at their headquarters at New York has introduced a wide range of physical fitness programmes for their employees which were initially meant for use by senior executives. The corporate HQ is located in an attractive setting, providing a gym, sauna, whirlpool and massage facilities. The atmosphere encourages the employees to take up physical fitness.

In the UK two health care insurance companies (BUPA and PPP) 'have promoted preventative measures - medical screening, stress management programmes, and occupational health advice - no doubt believing that a healthier work-force will mean fewer claims' (McKenna, 1994). The Marks and Spencer organisation, in London, have facilities such as gym, doctors, nurses, dentists, physiotherapists, osteopaths and health administrators. The company's deputy head of health services claimed that the service reduces absenteeism, increases the efficiency of the workforce and is an example of the commitment of the organisation to its employees (McKenna, 1994). DuPont has a scheme called 'Health Horizons'. A lifestyle questionnaire is completed by the employees and then analysed by computer. The employees are advised where to concentrate their efforts to improve their health. In addition, self help kits and incentives are available for the employees (McKenna, 1994).

However, there is very little scientific evidence on the evaluation of health promotion programmes in the UK, but in the USA, a number of programmes show impressive results. Doctors and other health care professionals could make a conscious effort to organize fitness training during lunch times or other non-work hours. Leisure activities provide relaxation and reduce the effect of work-stress. Regular breaks during working hours would give a chance to 're-charge the batteries' and help the doctors to unwind. Hospitals and general practices unable to implement this idea, due to limited space, may make arrangements with their local health clubs for using fitness programme facilities for doctors and other health care professionals. Although these programmes address some important issues on stress management, they do not always directly deal with the organizational reform issues which is beyond the scope of this book.

Counselling

An employee may seek help directly or be referred by his/her employer, to a counsellor, if he/she has a problem which can be solved by the counsellor. The giant copper corporation, Kennecott Corporation, introduced a counselling programme for employees in distress which produced a drop in absenteeism of nearly 60% in one year and a 55% reduction in medical costs (cited in Cooper et al 1988). The Post Office has introduced stress counsellors in two main metropolitan regions. In addition to helping the individuals to cope with stress in the workplace, they also identified the sources of stress in the workplace which may be causing problems. They carried out an evaluation of the effectiveness of the counselling simultaneously. Preliminary results, to assess the effect of the counselling on outcomes, showed that there was a significant difference between pre and post-counselling measures on anxiety and depression (Cooper et al 1989). "Sickness absence showed a decline of 60% from the sixth month period before, to the sixth month period after counselling".

It has been suggested that many doctors do not have their own general practitioner, and occupational health services within the NHS have been quoted as among the poorest in the UK (BMA, 1991). Therefore it is important that occupational health services should be upgraded and awareness should be raised for the need for such provision for all NHS staff. However, attempts have been made in the UK to provide support service for doctors suffering from stress at work (HMSO, 1975). The 'three wise men', is a committee which investigates complaints within the profession about doctors who exhibit difficulties in their functioning, such as drinking problems and drug addiction. This system has, however, tended to penalise and reprimand doctors rather than provide some form of coping support (HMSO, 1975). The General Medical Council is actively involved in providing some service to rehabilitate them. But without the establishment of a definite and formal support system, stress-related problems may continue among doctors.

The National Counselling service for sick doctors has handled 450 calls since its inception in 1985 (Rawnsley, 1989). Its services are open to all medical practitioners in the UK and calls are accepted from sick doctors, colleagues and spouses. It is funded by the Government and managed by a small independent committee of management which provides a humane and constructive approach to the sick doctor whose competence to practice has been eroded. In general practice, the FHSAs and Local Medical Committees (LMCs) may intervene when concern has been raised about a local colleague. Relatively small numbers of cases are dealt with by these statutory arrangements compared with the numbers handled by the counselling service (Rawnsley, 1989). National advisors are drawn from all branches of medicine, include 60 general practitioners and are distributed throughout the UK. When a call is received, the only detail taken at the centre is the area in which the general practitioner works. If the sick doctor is willing to accept help, the national advisor may undertake the task or call upon one of the 250 counsellors working for the service to become involved.

The National Association for Staff Support (NASS) is a registered charity consisting of professionals co-ordinating and developing staff support resources for all health care staff. They do not provide an individual counselling service but aim to identify and promote good staff practices. The Association has produced a number of reports on stress management within the health service and has contacts all over the country who provide help and advice on staff support services.

There may be substantial benefit in providing a counselling service and/or Employee Assistance Programme for doctors, and other health care professionals who find themselves under psychological pressure from their work. The National Counselling Service for Sick Doctors argued that doctors require 'special services' run through a network of independent regional bodies, as doctors tend to make little use of general health services unless they are very ill (Armstrong, 1997). Other services for doctors with mental illnesses include BMA counselling line, the British Doctors and Dentists Groups, the Sick Doctors Trust, Counsel for Sick Doctors and Overseas Doctors Health Counselling Panel.

Training

Adequate training needs to be provided to those during medical training years, and be continued during their career as well so that they can cope better with the stresses of medicine. It could be suggested that removing part of the factual load from the curriculum could allow the inclusion of topics such as communication skill, team work, stress management and administration. In the USA, a growing number of medical schools and residency programmes are providing courses for medical students to understand the pressures of the inherent susceptibility in medical practice before any serious problems develop (see Butterfield, 1988 for review).

As stated in the Edinburgh Declaration that medical education aims to produce doctors who will promote the health of all individuals, and efforts to introduce greater social awareness into medical schools have not been notably successful (World Federation for Medical Education, 1988). Recommendations were made to reform medical education (World Federation for Medical Education, 1988).

Failures are inevitable in the medical profession. Therefore, training should be provided in the techniques of coping with blame when there is a failure. However, it is important for doctors to learn to live with uncertainty and failure as some of the factors considered as inherent to the job may not be possible to alter.

Social support

Social support refers to the help or support from other human beings such as spouse, family, friends, neighbours, colleagues and acquaintances. Individuals with social support believe they are loved and cared for, esteemed and valued, and part of a social network that can provide goods or services and mutual defence in times of need (Cobb, 1976). Social support can reduce stress and improve health in three possible ways (House, 1981):

1 Social support can directly reduce stress level. For example, support from work colleagues can reduce interpersonal pressure at work.
2 Social support can improve health and well-being by raising resistance to illness.
3 Supportive relationships buffer the impact of stress on health and promote a sense of well-being.

The importance of social support in the work environment can not be overemphasized. Support in the work environment has been studied and found to be beneficial to the workers. Supportive behaviour of managers and co-workers can improve productivity, staff morale, and prevent several types of occupational stress. Creation of a network system is only possible if everyone in the organisations is willing to participate. It is therefore necessary to make the members aware of the benefits of such a system and then motivate them to participate in such a scheme. Motivation is required both at individual and organisational level.

Social support can be set up in different ways in primary and secondary care. All the different groups of professionals in primary care and secondary care would benefit from setting up a 'support network' system. This works by members of each profession (e.g. medical students, junior doctors, general practitioners, consultants) forming small groups. The number of individuals in each group will vary according to the number of people in that organization. A group of ten members could form five colleague pairs so that when a problem is experienced by a member, he/she can feel free to discuss it with a fellow colleague in a non-threatening and comfortable environment but, if a solution is not found, this pair may wish to involve one of the other pairs. Ultimately, the whole group may meet and try to find a solution. If all fails, then outside help may be required.

Support groups can also be set-up by mixing members from different categories of doctor. The group may have members with differing views on organizational and personal matters but these differences may soon be compromised once the aim of the group is perceived as helping each other. The group can meet regularly which will enable the members to explore the issues relating to stress; for example: identifying the causes of stress, ways of coping with particular stressors and coping with stress in long term basis.

Stress can be reduced by improving the relationships among the different members of the medical and other health care professional groups. Chapman (1993) examined the relationship between nurses' perceptions of collegial support and work stressors. The study concluded that identifying and reinforcing effective coping strategies and developing supporting relationships can enable a nurse to provide better nursing care. Anecdotal evidence suggests that school teachers are able to discuss their problems in the teachers' common room but doctors might not be open to each other about their problems in their work place. Support groups and peer counselling should be encouraged and formalised for all doctors and health care professionals. Hospitals and Family Health Services Authorities can help in establishing support groups for the doctors and other health care professionals. These meetings can provide opportunity to help each other to cope with stress. When the problem is severe, as in a sick doctor, professional help is required.

Social support is "giving and receiving". The ability to acquire the attitude for giving and receiving can be developed through learning. Individuals with similar interests may join self-help groups, including Alcoholic Anonymous (for individuals with drinking problems and their families), and other social interest groups.

A study in Tyneside, England was conducted to find out general practitioners' views regarding the need for a stress support service (Young and Spencer, 1996). The most popular options for the service was independently accessed counsellors and stress management groups which should be available to all doctors and their families. However, a range of options would be required to meet the variety of perceived needs, and these services should be made accessible to all doctors and their families.

A self-help group for general practitioners known as Doctors Support Network (DSN) began in early 1997. The focus of DSN is to permit doctors with mental health problems to provide each other support. The DSN co-ordinated by doctors who have experienced a breakdown. It provides a safe environment to share experiences and reduce fear and guilt. The meetings are held in London. It has the voluntary services of an occupational health physician. The supporters of occupational health services claim that this will pick up the early warning signals of stress.

Working women and dual career couples

Working women and dual career couples have special problems. Our study showed that women doctors experience additional stressors in comparison to their male counterparts (Rout and Rout, 1993, 1999). In a dual-career doctor family, the burden of on-call hours, sharing housework and childcare becomes complicated and stressful. Hence a balance has to be struck between working lives and personal lives. There are several ways in which the organizations can help to reduce stress amongst working women and dual career couples. Lewis and Cooper (1988) highlight a number of 'flexitime' approaches that organizations can provide for dual career couples. When spouses have non-traditional sex roles the flexitime system can be extremely helpful for both of the partners, reducing the stress of combining work and family (Lee, 1983, cited in Lewis and Cooper, 1988). For example, women doctors could use a system, which would allow them to come and go within the flexible time range set by the organization. A net number of working hours has to be met for a given period of time, and then people are free to choose their own working times. They may find it useful to follow the flexitime system, especially the 'flexiyear' system, adapted by several German firms in which a total number of working hours is decided for the whole year, and the employees are free to choose their own working time. This system allows the employees to chose to work less number of hours during school holidays, and makes the other activities easier. Some organisations can be flexible in allowing their employees to do the same job in their homes (Flexiplace). Other flexible working arrangements such as: part-time work, job sharing and career breaks can be considered by hospitals and practices.

Individual strategies

In addition to training, support and counselling there should be an increased awareness of individual strategies to improve 'personal fitness' for stress (for example, exercise, meditation, relaxation, cognitive restructuring and time management). Some of these are described below.

Meditation

The meaning of meditation is 'exercising the mind'. Individuals who meditate report being calm (as 'feelings of well-being'). They may appear calm and quiet, but remain quite alert at the same time. For centuries meditation has been used for mystical and religious reasons. There are many good articles on meditation theory and history (for example, Bond 1986; Leshan, 1975). Two Eastern approaches of meditation from Hindu philosophy are internalized into Western practice. These approaches, called Yantra and Mantra meditation, are derived from Hindu Sanskrit words. These can be exercised to induce relaxation and to explore self-awareness.

While practising Yantra meditation one has to adopt a visual image (such as a candle or an abstract shape) to exterminate distracting thoughts from the mind. The object of concentration can be anything. Because individuals differ in their intellectual make-up and therefore it is essential for them to choose an object with which they feel comfortable. In religious practice the object of meditation is God. However, ultimately the idea is to concentrate on one thing only at a particular time. Before practising Yantra meditation, people should be aware of any serious medical condition that they may have which might be aggravated by the Yantra meditation practice. Anecdotal evidence suggests that Yantra meditation can produce miracles. The following example shows:

> Once upon a time there lived a man in a small town near Himalayas, in India. He was very poor and had a large family to feed. One day the king announced that he would reward handsome wealth if anyone could remain submerged in the water of a specific cold pond. The water was ice cold and people thought nobody would ever survive even for a short while in the water. But this poor man was attracted to the wealth and decided to get in the water so that he could feed his family. People laughed at his cachectic body and thought that he wouldn't survive for a moment. However, the man was determined and he adopted his 'Yantra' meditation. He got in the water and remained submerged all night by gazing at

the candle light at the nearby temple. In the morning, people from all over came to the pond and were surprised to see him alive. The king came to greet this man and rewarded him as promised. When asked how he managed to keep himself alive, he replied that because of the strength of the 'Yantra' meditation he was able to survive. From that day the king himself started practising 'Yantra' meditation.

Mantra meditation deals with sounds and phrases rather than visual images. For example, a neutral word or a verse from a prayer is repeated again and again to aid concentration. Several Sanskrit words in yoga qualify as Mantras. For example, 'Ram, Syam, or Om'. Ram and Syam are names of Hindu Gods and 'Om' is regarded to be the basis of everything. Buddhists and Tibetan lamas understand 'Om' similarly. 'Om' is probably the most widely used of all Mantras.

Often the Mantras are practised along with fingering rosary beads which fix the meditator's attention. However, Mantras do not have to be sacred or religious. Researchers have shown that nonsense syllables or simple words like 'one' or 'calm' or 'relaxed', 'harmony' can be repeated by the meditator to produce relaxation experience and meditation (Petersen, 1979; Benson, 1980). Doctors and their family members could practice Mantra meditation without objecting to it on grounds of their religion. Attention should be given in controlling breathing when distracting thoughts disturb.

Transcendental meditation (TM) is a simplified version of Mantra meditation promoted by Maharishi Mahesh Yogi as a method of improving physical and mental health and reducing stress (Benson, 1984). Benson (1974) investigated TM and its impact upon stress reduction and developed another technique, named secular meditation, which duplicated the results of TM (i.e. drop in the rate of metabolic function - such as, reduced systolic, diastolic blood pressure, heart rate and respiratory response). Benson suggests that his approach of TM be continued for approximately 20 minutes and practised once or twice a day, but not within two hours of a meal. It is recommended that the relaxation response 'can act as a built-in method of counteracting the stresses of everyday living, which bring forth the fight-or-flight response' (Benson, 1974).

The 'purpose of relaxation training is to reduce the individual's arousal level and bring about a calmer state of affairs from both psychological and physiological perspectives. Psychologically, successful relaxation results in enhanced feelings of well-being, peacefulness, a sense of control, and a reduction in felt tension and anxiety: physiologically, decrease in blood pressure, respiration, and heart rate should take place' (Matteson and Ivancevich, 1987). There are several excellent books written by stress management consultants on relaxation and stress control. Relaxation is a skill to be learned and requires motivation, effort and commitment. There are simple relaxation techniques which anyone can practice.

Deep relaxation can help prevent the build up of tension, fatigue and anxiety. When the hypothalamus (part of the brain that controls stress-response) is stimulated by a variety of sensory impulses, it becomes highly charged. Then, each and every stressor could easily lead to stress-response. It is important to cut down the sensory impulses going to the brain by lying down, closing the eyes and deeply relaxing the body. By doing this both body and mind can return to a state of equilibrium and restore the balance. Using the deep relaxation method Patel and her colleagues (1973, 1975, 1987, 1985, 1988), in several studies, found a reduction in high blood pressure and the risk of having heart attack in the future and improved quality of life. The technique is based on yogic exercise.

In progressive muscle relaxation, individuals focus their attention on specific sets of muscles in the body, whilst alternately tensing and relaxing these muscles. Progressive relaxation was developed by Jacobson (1929, 1934). It is very effective in reducing stress. One of the reasons of muscle relaxation reducing psychological stress is that the method tends to arouse pleasant thoughts in the individual (Peveler and Johnston, 1986). It is essential to practice breathing co-ordination. One must breathe in a passive way without making any conscious effort to regulate the breathing. As the body relaxes the breathing pattern will automatically become regular. It is essential to pay attention while tensing and relaxing the muscles.

After mastering deep relaxation one can attempt to do momentary relaxation. This can be achieved in a few seconds without even closing the eyes. Before dealing with a stressful situation one can pause for a few seconds and let the body relax. Then come back to the situation while retaining the feeling of calmness.

Autogenic training

The meaning of autogenic is self-generating. The basic technique of autogenic training (Autogenic Regulation Training) was developed by Johannes Schultz, a German Psychiatrist, and utilized by Wolfgang Luthe (Schultz and Luthe, 1969). Individuals repeat a series of phrases mentally by giving themselves instructions to different parts of their body.

There are several benefits of autogenic regulation. For example, episodes of insomnia, tension headaches, and asthmatic attacks are reduced (Wittkower and Warnes, 1977; Rosa, 1976). Also, autogenic training practice regulates heart rate, reduces respiratory functioning and decreases blood pressure and muscle tension (Schultz and Luthe, 1959; Luthe, 1963; Luthe and Blumberger, 1977). Individuals who practise autogenic training report relaxation, peace, tranquillity, and well-being (Bailey, 1985). The response generated by autogenic training appears to be psycho-physiologically similar to Benson's relaxation response (Bakal, 1979; Benson, 1980). Self-hypnosis plays an important role in autogenic training (Ulett and Peterson, 1965). Autogenic training is described by Quick and Quick (1984) as a method of self-hypnosis which 'emphasizes the development of individual control over physiologic process through organ and symptom specific exercises'.

Biofeedback

Biofeedback is a technique in which instruments are used to help individuals in controlling functions of the autonomic nervous system. Body signals can be displayed by various means (for example, lights, sounds). Whichever way one chooses the body signals to be displayed, the aim is to enable the individual to connect the internal change to a behaviour or a thought. For example, an individual monitors an auditory signal of his/her heart rate or muscle tension and tries with different thoughts and feelings to show the heart rate or to reduce the muscle tension. When the individual recognises the feelings associated with decreased heart rate or muscle tension, the equipment is removed and the individual learns to control his/her own heart rate or muscle tension.

Biofeedback, autogenic training, progressive relaxation and meditation are similar techniques. Autogenic training, meditation and progressive relaxation decrease arousal and reduce the sympathetic nervous system activity, while the individual relaxes, but with biofeedback, the individual lowers certain physiological measures with the aid of an instrument. This in turn lowers arousal and prolongs relaxation. Biofeedback training has been used as a method for stress management by helping individuals learn to relax specific muscles (Quick and Quick, 1984). However, it is suggested that one needs to combine biofeedback with lifestyle change and cognitive coping strategies to obtain satisfactory long-term results (Rice, 1992).

Systematic desensitization

Systematic desensitization was developed by Joseph Wolpe (1958, 1973). This is a method for reducing stress, and is based on the view of classical conditioning. This method involves a process of reversing the associations that have been established previously between some environmental event and the stress response (Rimm and Masters, 1979). This method is used in dealing with specific stress reactions such as phobias and anxiety. Desensitization means removal of the sensitizing power of a feared object.

Stress inoculation training

Stress inoculation training approach was developed by Meichenbaum (1979). It is a cognitive approach to the management of stress, and achievement of personal goals (Meichenbaum and Cameron, 1983; Meichenbaum and Turk, 1982). Stress inoculation occurs in stages.

1. Conceptualization - During this phase the individual understands the nature or 'causes' of stress. This understanding occurs through discussions between the therapist and the client.

2. Skill acquisition and rehearsal - During this phase, the individual learns behavioural and cognitive skills (For example, he/she may learn relaxation and desensitization, cognitive re-definition, social skills training), and practises these skills.

3. Application and follow-through - During this phase the individual applies the learnt coping skills in the real world.

Cognitive restructuring

Cognitive restructuring is a technique by which stress-provoking thoughts or beliefs are changed with more constructive ones which can promote individuals' well-being, (Mahoney and Auener, 1977). The most widely used technique for changing irrational cognitions was developed by Albert Ellis (1962). This approach to cognitive restructuring is called Rational Emotive Therapy (RET). According to RET, stress often arises from 'irrational beliefs' or faulty training. Ellis (1962) described A-B-C-D-E paradigm to help the individual in disputing his/her irrational beliefs and construct healthier alternatives.

Constructive self-talk

Researchers believe that a 'constructive self-talk' helps people cognitively to reappraise stressful situations (Quick and Quick, 1984). Quick and Quick, (1984) describe this as 'intermittent mental monologue'. When an individual engages in 'negative self-talk', he/she only spends his/her energy, but achieves nothing and continues to maintain the stress. On the other hand, if the individual engages in 'constructive self-talk', he/she can achieve positive results. It has been suggested that constructive self-talk is not just positive thinking but a form of guided self-dialogue (Meichenbaum, 1985). The therapist encourages the person to recognise his/her negative self-talk. When it is recognised, it is written down sentence by sentence. Then an alternative to negative self-talk sentences are developed, the opposite to each original sentence.

Managing Type A behaviour

Type A behaviour pattern was discussed as a moderator of stress response and a type A questionnaire was presented in chapter 2 for you to find out the extent of your type A behaviour. If the doctors and their spouses feel that their score inclines towards type A, they could consider recommendations directed at managing type A behaviour pattern.

Type A behaviour modification programmes, with both CHD patients and healthy individuals, have shown significant reduction in serum cholesterol levels and blood pressure, lower frequencies of subsequent CHD, increased work productivity and improved family relationships (Rahe et al 1975; Chesney and Rosenman, 1980; Suinn, 1976). However, Friedman and Rosenman suggest that Type A behaviour should be managed rather than changed, to minimise the health risk associations involved.

Friedman and Rosenman (1974) recommend a number of 'drills against hurry sickness', which they claim work for their type A patients. Doctors and their spouses of Type A behaviour may find those suggestions helpful coping strategies.

Stress diary

It might be helpful to keep a stress diary to be able to identify precisely those individuals or related events that may be causing stress or tension. You could maintain a stress diary for days, weeks or months, noting all activities. This will provide information about the type of incident or person or situation that causes the individual most difficulty. Additionally, you should record your response to stress, i.e. what you did and finally think in retrospect what you should have done. An awareness of this should help the doctors and their spouses to develop an action plan to minimise or eliminate the stressors. At the end of the week/s you could review the incidents and people involved which caused the most stress and try to isolate particular events and specific people who consistently seem to be implicated in stressful work experiences; systematically think through the options or alternative methods of coping. You could set aside some time to analyse specifically the sources of problem and find out alternative coping strategies suitable to deal with future problems. It may be difficult to change certain things in life but it is worth trying in terms of long term personal happiness and effectiveness.

Developing a sense of humour

The idea of developing a sense of humour in life, to combat stress, may sound sceptical, but a true story of Norman Cousins proves how humour can have a powerful effect on our mind and body. Cousins (1979) was crippled by an incurable disease (i.e. autoimmune disease). He asked his doctor about prognosis. The doctor gave a disappointing opinion that his chances of recovery were extremely poor. He took a constructive view and wanted to manage his own therapy. He watched comedy movies and the nurses read him humour books. He recovered within a short time. Norman thought that his laughter contributed to his recovery. Although there was scepticism about Norman's claim at that time, researchers now believe that laughter can influence changes in our body functioning which improve the circulation, digestion and reduce muscle tension. These activities are the opposite of stress responses. Therefore, it may be appropriate to have laughter in our daily life.

Stress management course/stress awareness pack

While there are various stress management courses available; the choice of choosing a course depends on individual's preference, between residential/non residential courses or in-house stress management courses. In addition to these valuable courses, there are also stress awareness packs (of how stress can be manifested in themselves and others) available tailored for specific professions, which would help to understand the problem. Once the employees are aware of the stress symptoms in them, they can do something about them. For example, they can join a stress management training programme or try to modify the job stress factors. These stress management training courses can be attended by doctors and their spouses outside their organization. This might help to get rid of prejudice that is inherent in the attitude of stress. Then they can all try to tackle the problems.

Conclusions

This concluding chapter has outlined suggestions for the problems that doctors and their families encounter. Also individual and organisational stress management strategies were considered, as these are relevant in any stress management programme. Some of these organisational strategies have been tried in industry with success. NHS is rapidly turning into business style organisation. Therefore there is a need for doctors to adopt some of the suggestions given in this chapter which may provide a great sense of achievement and satisfaction, and less stressful work life. This is now the appropriate time for organisations to be redesigned to suit doctors and other health-care professionals of the future.

Removing the sources of stress is the best solution to alleviate stress but there are several circumstances where it is impossible to change the situation. Therefore one has to learn to live with it. There are some stressors for which no simple solutions can be found. In these circumstances if the doctors and the family members practise some individual stress management strategies (e.g. relaxation, meditation) they are more likely to be able to live with the stress. However, this book may help doctors and their families to identify stress in their lives and learn to control this with the help of others.

The way forward

The main limitation of our studies and other studies quoted from the literature is that the data collected were self-reported and cross-sectional. Nevertheless, psychological and physiological illnesses are largely evolutionary in nature and greater emphasis on longitudinal studies is now needed to understand clearly the processes involved. Future research on stress in doctors and their families clearly needs to be prospective. What is required now is the implementation and evaluation of prevention of stress programmes. Information about doctors' personal and family psychiatric history, their social support system and methods of dealing with stress need to be analysed. Considering the high incidence of depression among doctors further research could include psychiatric history, which may be helpful in determining whether depressive reactions are situational or endogenous. How these mental conditions affect personal and professional development and patient care remain an area of study. Stress must be recognised in relation to the ability of the doctors (their spouses and children), to tolerate it, the personality of the individual doctor and the way he or she perceives and interacts with the environment.

A larger study is now being conducted by the authors in order to investigate these findings further.

References

Aasland, U.G., Olff, M., Falkum, E., Schweder, T. and Ursin, H. (1997), Health complaints and job stress in Norwegian physicians: the use of an overlapping questionnaire design. *Social Science and Medicine*, 45, (11), pp 1515-29.

a'Brook, M.F. (1973), Mental stress at work. *The Practitioner*, 210, pp 500-6.

a'Brook, M.F. (1990), Psychosis and depression. *The Practitioner*, 234, pp 992-3.

Adey, C. (1987), Stress: who cares? *Nursing Times*, 28th January, pp 52-3.

Agas, M., Coulter, A., Mant. D., et al (1991), Patient participation in general practice: who participates. *British Journal of General Practice*, 41, pp 198-200.

Albrecht, K. (1979), *Stress and the Manager. Making it work for you*. Prentice-Hall: New Jersey.

Alfredson, L. Spetz, C.L. and Theorell, T. (1985), Type of occupation and near future hospitalisation for myocardial infarction and some other diagnosis, *International Journal of Epidemiology*, 14, pp 378-88.

Allen, I. (1988), *Any Room at the Top? A Study of Doctors and their Careers*, Policy Studies Institute: London.

Allibone, A., Oakes, D. and Shannon, H.S. (1981), The health and health care of doctors. *Journal of the Royal College of General Practitioners*, 31, pp 728-34.

AMA Council on Scientific Affairs (1986), *Results and implications of the AMA, American Physicians Association, Physicians Mortality Project*: Stage II.

Angel M. (1981), Women in medicine beyond prejudice. *The New England Journal of American Medical Womens Association*, 304 (19), pp 1161-3.

Anslinger H. J.(1957), Interview. *Modern Medicine*, 25, pp 170.

Anwar, M (1981), *'Between two cultures': A story of the relationships between generations in the Asian community in Britain*, CRE: London.

Appleton, K. House, A. and Dowell, A. (1998), A survey of job satisfaction, sources of stress and psychological symptoms among general practitioners in Leeds. *British Journal of General Practice*, 48, (428), pp 1059-63.

Armstrong, E. (1997), We help mentally ill GPs; *Medical Monitor*, 20, August : 15.

Baggott, R. (1991), *Health and health care in Britain*. The Macmillan Press: London.

Bailey, R.D. (1985), *Coping with Stress in Caring*. Blackwell Scientific Publications: London.

Bain, J. (1991), General practice and the new contract: Reaction and impact. *British Medical Journal*, 302, pp 1183-6.

Bakal, D. (1979), *Psychology and Medicine*. Tavistock: London.

Ballard, R. and Ballard, C., (1979), 'The development of South Asian settlements in Britain'. In J.L.Watson (eds), *Between two cultures*, Basil Blackwell: Oxford.

Barefoot, J.C., Dahlstrom, W.G. and Williams, R.B. (1983), Hostility, CHD incidence, and total mortality: A 25 year follow up study of 255 physicians. *Psychosomatic Medicine*, 45, (1): pp 59-63.

Barker MG. (1981), *The doctor's family*, Rendell short lecture 1980, April, in the service of medicine, supplement.

Barrera, M., Jr., and Baca, L.M. (1990), Recipient reaction to social support: Contributions of enacted support, conflicted support and network orientation. *Journal of Social and Personal Relationship*, 7, pp 541-51.

Bates, E. (1982), Doctors and spouses speak: Stress in medical practice. *Society Health and Illness*, 4.

Beecham, L. (1999), UK Consultants act to limit spiralling workload. *British Medical Journal*, 318; 896.

Bennet G. (1979), *Patients and their Doctors.* Ballière Tindall: London.

Bennet, G. (1982), Sick doctors - ourselves. *Journal of Postgraduate Medical Practice,* 24, pp 1621-31.

Benson, H. (1974), Your innate asset for combating stress. *Harvard Business Review.* 52 (4), pp 49-60.

Benson, H. (1980), *The Relaxation Response.* Fount Paperbacks, Collins: Glasgow.

Benson, H. (1984), *Beyond the Relaxation Response.* Time Books: New York.

Bickel J. (1988), Women in medical education: A status report. *New England Journal of Medicine,* 319, pp 579-84.

Billings, A.G. and Moos, R.H. (1982), Work stress and the stress buffering roles of work and family resources. *Journal of Occupational Behaviour,* 3, pp 213-32.

Billings, A. G. and Moos, R.H. (1981), The role of coping responses and social resources in attenuating the stress of life events. *Journal of Behavioural Medicine,* 4, pp 139-57.

Bird, C. (1979), *The two paycheque marriage: how women at work are changing life in America.* Rawshon Wade: New York.

Bissel, L. and Jones, R.W. (1976), The alcoholic physician: a survey. *American Journal of Psychiatry,* 133, p 1142.

Bjorksten, O., Sutherland, S., Miller, C. and Stewart, T. (1983), Identification of medical student problems and comparison with those of other students. *Journal of Medical Education,* 58, pp759-67.

Blackly, P.H., Disher, W. and Roduner, G. (1968), *Suicide by physicians.* Bull Suicidology, December, pp 1-18.

Blohmke, M., Schaefer, H., Abel, H., Depner, R., Koschorreck, B. and Steizer, O. (1969), Medizinische and Soziale Befunde bei koro-naren Herzkrankheiten. *Munchener Medizinische Wochenschrift,* pp 701-10.

Bloomfield, H.H., Cain M.P., Jaffe, D.T. and Kory, R.B. (1975), *TM - Discovering Inner Energy and Overcoming Stress.* Dell: New York.

Boffetta, P. and Garfinkel, L. (1990), Alcohol drinking and mortality among men enrolled in an American Cancer Society prospective

study. *Epidemiolopy*, 1, pp 342-8.
Bojar, S. (1971), Psychiatric problems of medical students. In G.B. Blaine and C.C. McArthur (eds), *Emotional problems of the students*. Appleton - Century Crofts: New York. pp 350-63.
Bolger, N., Delongis, A., Kessler, R.C. and Wethington, E. (1990), The microstructure of daily role-related stress in married couples. In J. Eckenrod and S. Gore (eds), *Stress between work and family*; Plenum Press: New York, pp 95-115.
Bond, M. (1986), *Stress and Self-Awareness*, Heinemann: London.
Bowman, M.A. and Allen, D.I. (1990), *Stress and women physicians* (second Ed), Springer-Veriag: New York.
Bramness, J.G., Fixdal, T.C. and Vaghum, P. (1991), Effect of medical school stress on the mental health of medical students in early and late clinical curriculum. *Acta Psychiatrica Scandinavia;* 84, pp 340-345.
Brannen, J., Meszaros, G., Moss, P. and Poland, G. (1994), *Employment and Family Life, A Review of Research in the UK (1980-1994)*, Institute of Education, University of London: London.
Brief, A.P., Rude, D.E. and Rabinowitz, S. (1983), The impact of type A behaviour pattern on subjective workload and depression. *Journal of Occupational Behaviour*, 4, pp 157-64.
British Medical Association (1991), Reforms sap doctors' morale. *BMA News Review*, June.
British Medical Association (1992), Stress and the medical profession. *British Medical Association*: London.
British Medical Association (1993), The morbidity and mortality of the medical profession. *British Medical Association, Board of Science and Education*: London.
British Medical Association (1996), Doctors under Stress. *BMA News Review*, 22, pp 32-4.
Brown, J.B. (1992), Female family doctors: their work and well-being. *Family Medicine*, 24 (8), pp 591-5.
Bruhn, J.C., McCrady, K.E. and Du Plessis, A. (1968), Evidence of 'emotional drain' preceding death from myocardial infarction. *Psychiatry Digest*, 29, pp 34-40.

Buchan J. and Stock J. (1990), *Early Careers of General Practitioners. Institute of Manpower Studies*, University of Sussex: Brighton.

Bulstrode, C. (1991), Vice-versa:Consultant becomes junior. *British Medical Journal*, 303, July, pp 255-6.

Burke, R.I. and Belcourt, M.L. (1974), Managerial role stress and coping responses. *Journal of Business Adminstration*, 5, pp 55-68.

Burke, R.J., Weir, T. and Duwors, R.E. (1979), Type A behaviour of administrators and wives' reports of marital satisfaction and well being. *Journal of Applied Psychology*, 64 pp 57-65.

Burke, R.J., Weir, T and Duwors, R.E. (1980), Work demands on administrators and spouse well being. *Human Relations*, 33, pp 253-78.

Burke, R.J. and Greenglass, E.R. (1987), Work and family. In C. Cooper and I. Robertson (Eds), *International Review of Industrial and Organizational Psychology*, Wiley: New York, pp 273-320.

Butterfield, P.S. (1988), The stress of residency, *Archives of Internal Medicine*, 148, pp 1428-35.

Caplan L (1971), Organisational stress and individual strain: A social-psychosocial study of risk factors in coronary disease among administrators, engineers and scientists. Ann Arbor, Research Centre for Group Dynamics: Michigan.

Caplan, R.P. (1994), Stress, anxiety and depression in hospital consultants, general practitioners and senior health service managers. *British Medical Journal*, 309, pp 1261-3.

Cartwright, L.K. (1977), Continuity and non continuity in the careers of a sample of young physicians. *Journal of the American Medical. Women's Association*, 32(9), pp 316-21.

Chambers, R. (1992), The health and lifestyle of general practitioners and teachers. *Occpational Medicine*, 42, pp 69-78.

Chambers R. and Campbell, I. (1996), Gender differences in general practitioners at work. *British Journal of General Practice*, 46 (406) pp 291-93.

Chambers, R. and Belcher, J. (1993), Comparison of health and lifestyle of general practitioners and teachers. *British Journal of General Practice*, 43, pp 378-82.

Chapman, J. (1993), Collegial support linked to reduction of job stress, *Nursing Management,* 24 (5), pp 52-4.

Charles, S.C., Wilbert, J.R. and Franke, K.J. (1985), Sued and non-sued physicians: self-reported reactions to malpractice litigations. *American Journal of Psychiatry,* 142, pp 437-40.

Check, J.V.P. and Dyck, D.G. (1986), Hostile, aggression and Type A behaviour. *Journal of Personality and Individual Differences,* 7 (6), pp 819-27.

Chesney, M.A. and Rosenman, R.H. (1980), Type A behaviour in the Work Setting in C .L. Cooper and R. Payne (eds), *Current Concerns in Occupational Stress.* John Wiley: Chichester.

Clark, D.C. and Zeldow, P.B. (1988), Vicissitudes of depressed mood during four years of medical school, *Journal of the American Medical Association,* 260, pp 2521-8.

Cobb, S. (1976), Social support as a moderator of life stress. *Psychosomatic Medicine,* 38, pp 300-14.

Cobourn, D. and Joviafaf, A.V. (1975), Perceived sources of stress among first year medical students. *Journal of Medical Education,* 55, pp 590-5.

Cooke, R.A and Rousseau, D.M. (1984), Stress and strain from family role and work - role expectations. *Journal of Applied Psychology,* 67, pp 361-9.

Coombs, R.H. and Hovanessian, H.C. (1988), Stress in the role constellation of female resident physicians. *Journal of the American Medical Women's Association,* 43, pp 21-26.

Cooper, C.L. (1980), Work stress in white and blue collar jobs. *Bulletin of British Psychological Society,* 33, pp 49-51.

Cooper, C.L. (1982), *Executive Families Under Stress.* Prentice-Hall: New Jersey.

Cooper, C.L., Cooper, R.D and Eaker, L.H. (1988), *Living with Stress.* Penguin: Harmondsworth.

Cooper, C.L., Reynolds, P. and Sadri, G. (1989), Stress counselling in industry: *The Post Office experience.* Paper presented at The Annual Conference of The British Psychological Society, March: St. Andrews.

Cooper, C.L., Rout, U. and Faragher, B. (1989), Mental health, job satisfaction and job stress among general practitioners. *British*

Medical Journal, 298, pp 366-70.

Coser, L. (1974), *Greedy Institutions*. Free Press: New York.

Cousins, N. (1979), *Anatomy of an Illness*, Bantam Books: New York.

Crosby, F. (1984), Satisfaction and domestic life. In M. D. Lee and R. N. Kanungo (eds), *Management of Work and Personal Life*, Praeger: New York, pp 168-193.

Cull, A. (1991), Studying stress in care givers : art or science. *British Journal of Cancer*, 64, pp 981-4.

Davidson, M.J. and Cooper, C.L. (1984), Occupational stress in female managers: a comparative study. *Journal of Management Studies*, 21 (2), pp 185-205.

Davidson, J.(1978), *Effective Time Management*. Human Science Press: New York.

Davidson, M. (1997), *The black and ethnic woman manager*. Paul Chapman Publishing Ltd: London.

Davies, K. (1989), *Women and time: Weaving the sounds of everyday life*. University of Lund: Sweden.

De Frank, R.S. and Cooper, C.L. (1987), Worksite stress management interventions: Their effectiveness and conceptualisation. *Journal of Managerial Psychology*, 2 (1), pp 4-10.

Dewe, P. (1991) Measuring work stressors: the role of frequency, duration, and demand. *Work and Stress*, 5, pp 77-91.

Dewe, P.J. (1987), Identifying the causes of nurses' stress. *Work and Stress*, 1 (1).

Dickinson, F.G. and Martin, L.W. (1956), Physician mortality, 1949-1951 Bureau of Medical Economic Research. *Journal of the American Medical Association*, 162, pp 1462-8.

Dilworth-Anderson, P., Burton, L. and Turner, W. (1993), The importance of values in the study of culturally diverse families. *Family Relations*, 42 (3), pp 238-42.

Doll, R. and Peto, R. (1976), Mortality in relation to smoking: 20 years observations on male British doctors. *British Medical Journal*, 2, pp 1525-36.

Drury, B (1991), Sikh girls and the maintenance of an ethnic culture; *New Community*, 17(3), pp 387-99, April.

Dublin, L.I. and Spiegelman, M. (1947), The longevity and mortality of American physicians, 1938-1942. *Journal of the American Medical Association*, 134, pp 1211-15.

Dublin, L.I. and Spiegelman, M. (1948), Mortality of medical specialists, 1938-1942. *Journal of the American Medical Association*, 137, p 1519.

Ducker, D.G. (1980), The effects of two sources of role strain on women physicians. *Sex Roles*, 6, pp 549-59.

Elli, A (1962), the basic clinical theory of rational emotive theory. In A. Ellis and R. Grieger (eds), *Handbook of rational emotive therapy*. New York: Springer.

Elliot, C.M. (1981), Women physicians of workers. *Journal of the American Medical Women's Association*, 36, pp 105-8.

Elliot, F.R. (1978), The conflict between work and family in hospital medicine. *Health Trends*, 10, pp 17-8.

Epstain, R.K. (1983), The new total woman. *Working Woman*, pp 100-103.

Everson, R.B. and Fraumeni, I.F. (1975), Mortality among medical students and young physicians. *Journal of Medical Education*, 30 (8), pp 809-11.

Fain, R.M. and Schreier, R.A. (1989), Disaster, stress and the doctor. *Medical Education*, 23, pp 91-6.

Falkenberg, L.E. (1987), Employee fitness programme: Their impact on the employee and organisation. *Academy of Management Review*, 12 (3), pp 511-2.

Fine, C. (1981), *Married to Medicine: An Intimate Portrait of Doctors' Wives*. Atheneum: New York.

Fine, M. (1993), Current approaches to understanding family diversity. *Family Relations*, 42 (3), pp 235-7.

Firth, J.A. (1986), Levels and sources of stress in medical students. *British Medical Journal*, 292, pp 1177-80.

Firth-Cozens, J. (1990), Sources of stress in women junior house officers. *British Medical Journal*, 301, pp 89-91.

Firth-Cozens, J. (1987), Emotional distress in junior house officers. *British Medical Journal*, 295, pp 533-5.

Firth-Cozens, J. (1997), Predicting stress in general practitioners: 10 year follow-up postal survey. *British Medical Journal*, 315, pp 34-5.

Floderus, B. (1974), *Psychosocial factors in relation to coronary heart disease and associated risk factors*. Nord HygTidsskr: 6.

Folkman, S. and Lazarus, R. S. (1980), An analysis of coping in middle-aged community sample. *Journal of Health and Social Behaviour*, 21, pp 219-39.

Friedman, H.S. and Booth-Kewley, S. (1987), The 'disease-prone personality': A Meta-analytic view of the construct. *American Psychologist*. 42(6), pp 539-55.

Friedman, M. and Rosenman, R.H. (1974), *Type A behaviour and your heart*. Knopf: New York.

Friedman, R.C., Kornfield, D.S. and Bigger, T.J. (1973), Psychological problems associated with sleep deprivation in interns. *Journal of Medical Education*, 48, pp 346-41.

Gabbard, G., Merringer, M.D, and Coyne, L. (1987), Sources of conflict in the medical marriage. *American Journal of Psychiatry*, 144, pp 567-72.

Gabbard, G. (1985), The role of compulsiveness in the normal physician. *Journal of the American Medical Association*, 254, pp 2926-29.

Gaensbauer, T.J. and Mizner, G.L. (1980), Developmental stresses in medical education. *Psychiatry*, 43, 60-70.

Garvey, M. and Tuason. V.B. (1979), Physician marriages. *Journal of Clinical Psychiatry*, 40, pp 129-31.

Gerber, A. (1983), *Married to their career and family dilemmas in doctors' lives*, Tavistock: New York.

Ghodse, A.H. and Howse K. (1994), Substance use of medical students: a nationwide survey. *Health Trends*, 26 (3), pp 85-88.

Ghuman, P. (1994), *Coping with two cultures: British Asian and Indo-Canadian Adolescents*. Multilingual Matters Ltd: Clevenon.

Golding, J.F. and Cornish, A.M. (*1987),* Personality and lifestyle in medical students: some psychopharmacological aspects. *Psychology and Health*, pp 287-301.

Gomberg, E.S. (1979), Problems with alcohol and other drugs. In E.S. Gomberg and V. Franks (eds), *Gender and disordered behaviour*. Brunner/Mazel: New York, pp 204-40.

Goode, W.J. (1960), A theory of role strain. *American Sociological Review*, pp 25, 483-496.

Goodman U. (1975), The longevity and mortality of American physicians: 1969-1973. *Millbank Memorial Fund Quarterly*, 53, p 353.

Gore, S. (1978), The effects of social supports in moderating the health consequences of unemployment. *Journal of Health and Social Behaviour*, 19, pp 157-65.

Gove, W.R. and Tudor, J. (1973), About sex roles and mental illness. *American Journal of Sociology*, 78, pp 812-835.

Grant, I. and DuRoss, D.J. (1984), Expected rewards of practice and personal-life priorities of women and male medical students. *Sociological Focus*, 17, pp 87-104.

Gray, J.P. (1982), The doctor's family: Some problems and solutions. *Journal of the Royal College of General Practitioners*, 32, pp 75-9.

Green, R.C., Carroll, G.I. and Buxton, W.D. (1976), Drug addiction among physicians. The Virginia Experience. *Journal of the American Medical Association*, 236 (12), pp 1372-5.

Greenhaus, J.H. and Parasuraman, S. (1994), Work-family conflict, social support and well-being. In M. Davidson and R. Burke (eds.), *Women in management. Current Research Issues*. Paul Chapman Publishing Ltd. London.

Grol, R., Mokking, H., Smits, A., Van, Eijk, J., Beek, M., Mesker, P. and Mesker-Niesten, J. (1985), Work satisfaction of general practitioners and the quality of patient care. *Family Practice*, 2, pp 128-35.

Gross, E.B. (1997), Gender differences in physician stress: Why the discrepant findings. *Women and Health*, 26 (3), pp 1-15.

Hale, R. and Hudson, L. (1992), The Tavistock study of young doctors: Report of the plot phase. *British Journal of Hospital Medicine*, 47 (6), pp 452-64.

Hall A. (1988), Medical marriage: no bed of roses. *British Medical Journal*, 296, pp 152-153.

Hall, D.T. and Goodale, J.G. (1986), *Human resource management: Strategy, design and implementation.* Glenview, IL: Scott Foresman.

Health Update No. 3 (1993) Alcohol Health Education Authority: London.

Heins M. Smock S. et al (1977), Comparison of the productivity of women and men physicians. *Journal of the American Medical Association,* 237(23), pp 2514-7.

Heins M. Smock S., Martindale L., Jacobs J and Stein M. (1977), Comparison of the productivity of women and men physicians. *Journal of the American Medical Association,* 237(23), pp 2514-7.

Hendrix, W.H. Spencer, B.A. and Gibson, G.S. (1994), Organisational and extra-organisational factors affecting stress, employee well-being and absenteeism for male and females. *Journal of Business and Psychology,* 9, 103-28.

Hingley, P. and Cooper, C.L. (1986), *Stress and the Nurse Manager.* John Wiley and Sons: Chichester.

HMSO (1994), *Nutritional Aspects of Cardiovascular Disease,* Department of Health: London.

HMSO (1975), *Report of the Committee of Inquiry into the Regulation of the Medical Profession.* A.W. Merrison.

HMSO (1978), *Occupational Mortality.* The Registrar General's decennial supplement for England and Wales (1970-72): London.

HMSO (1996), *Labour Market Trends*: London.

Horder E. (1982) Stress in the GP's family. In *Royal College of General Practitioners, 1982 Members' Reference Book,* RCGP: London.

House, J.S. (1981), *Work Stress and Social Support.* Addition-Wessley: USA.

Howie, R.G.R., Porter, A.M.D. and Forbes, J.F. (1989), Quality and use of time in general practice: widening the discussion. *British Medical Journal,* 298, pp 1008-10.

Hurrell, J.J. and Kroes, W.H.(1975), *Stress Awareness.* National Institute for Occupational Safety and Health: Cincinnati.

Irvine, J. Lyle, R.C. and Allon, R. (1982), Type A personality as psychopathology: Personality correlates and an abbreviated scoring system. *Journal of Psychosomatic Research*, 26, pp183-9.

Ivancevich, J.M., Matteson, M.T., Freedman, S.M. and Phillips, J.S. (1990), Worksite stress management interventions. *American Psychologist*, February, pp 252-61.

Jacobson, N.S. (1978), 'Review of the Research on the Effectiveness of Marital Therapy'. In *Marriages and Marital Therapy: Psychoanalytic, Behavioral and Systemic Theory Perspectives*. (eds.) Thomas J. Paolino and Barbara S. McCrady, Brunner/Mazel: New York, pp 395-444.

Jacobson, E. (1929), *Progressive Relaxation*. The University of Chicago Press: Chicago.

Jacobson, E. (1934), *You must relax*. Whittlesey House: New York.

Jenkins, C.D., Rosenman, R.H. and Friedman, M. (1967), Development of an objective psychological test for the determination of the coronary-prone behaviour pattern in employed men. *Journal of Chronic Diseases*, 20, pp 371-9.

Jenkins, D. (1971), Psychological and social precursors of Coronary Disease. *New England Journal of Medicine*, 284 (6), pp 307-17.

Jones, R.K. (1977), A study of 100 physician psychiatric in-patients. *American Journal of Psychiatry*, 134, (10), pp 1119-23.

Karasek, R., Gardell, B. and Lindell, J.(1987), Work and non-work correlates of illness and behaviour in male and female Swedish white-collar workers. *Journal of Occupational Behaviour*, 8, pp 187-207.

Karasek, R.A. Jr. (1979), Job demands, job decision latitude and mental strain: implications for job re-design. *Administrative Science Quarterly*, 24, pp 285–308.

Kasl, S.V. (1973), Mental health and work environment. An examination of the evidence. *Journal of Occupational Medicine*, 15, pp 506-15.

King, M.B., Cockcroft, A. and Gooch, C. (1992), Emotional distress in doctors : sources, effects and help sought. *The Royal Society of Medicine*, 85, pp 605-8.

Kitwood, T. (1983), '*Self-conception among young British Asian Muslims: Confrontation of a Stereotype*'. John Wiley and Sons Ltd: Chichester.

Knight, J.A. (1981), *Doctor-To-Be:Coping with the Trials and*

Triumphs of Medical School. Appleton-Century-Crofts: New York.

Kobasa, S.C. (1979), Stressful life events, personality and health : an enquiry into hardiness. *Journal of Personality and Social Psychology,* 37, pp 1-11.

Kobasa, S.C. and Puccetti, M. (1983), Personality and social resources in stress resistance. *Journal of Personality and Social Psychology;* 45, pp 839-50.

Kuna, D.J. (1975), Meditation and work. *Vocational Guidance Quarterly,* 23 (4), pp 342-6.

Kurian, G (1986), 'Intergenerational integration with special reference to Indian families. Special Issue: The family'; *Indian Journal of Social Work,* April, 47 (1), pp 39-49.

LaRocco, J.M. and Jones, A.P. (1978), Co-worker and leader support as moderators of stress-strain relationships in work situations, *Journal of Applied Psychology,* 63 (5), pp 629-34.

Lazarus, A.A. (1981), *The Practice of Multimodal Therapy.* Mcgraw-Hill: New York.

Leserman, J. (1981), *Men and women in medical school.* Praeger: New York.

Leshan, L. (1975), *How to Meditate.* Bantam Books: New York.

Levita, Z. (1995), Living with pressure:exploring stress and coping amongst general practitioners. *Primary Care Management,* 5 (6), pp 3-6.

Lewis, S. and Cooper, C.L. (1987), Stress in two earner couples and stage in the life cycle. *Journal of Occupational Psychology,* 60, pp 289-303.

Lewis, S. and Cooper, C.L. (1988), The transition to parenthood in dual-career couples. *Psychological Medicine,* 18, pp 477-486.

Lieberman, M. A. (1982), The effects of social support on response to stress. In L. Goldberger and L. Breznitz (eds), *Handbook of stress.* Free Press: New York.

Lloyd, C. and Gartrell, N.K. (1984), Psychiatric symptoms in medical students. *Comprehensive Psychiatry,* 25, pp 552-65.

Lloyd, G (1982), I am an alcoholic. *British Medical Journal,* 285, pp 785-6.

Long, J. and Porter, K.L. (1984), Multiple roles of midlife women: a case for new directions in theory, research and policy. In G. Braunch and J. Brooks-Gunn (eds), *Women in Midlife* (109-160), Plenum Press: New York.

Luthe, W. (1963), Autogenic state and autogenic shift. *Acta Psychotherapeutica Psychosomatica*, 11, pp 1-13.

Luthe, W. and Blumberger, S.R. (1977), Autogenic therapy. In E.D. Whittkower and H. Warnes (eds), *Psychosomatic Medicine: Its Clinical Applications*. Harper and Row: London.

Maheux, B. Dufort, F. and Beland, F. (1988), Professional and sociopolitical attitudes of medical students: Gender differences reconsidered. *Journal of the American Medical Women's Association*, 43 : 73-6.

Mahoney, M.J. and Avener, M. (1977), Psychology of the elite athlete: An exploratory study. *Cognitive Therapy and Research*, 1, pp 135-41.

Makin, P.J., Rout, U. and Cooper C.L. (1988), Job satisfaction and occupational stress in general pracitioners: A pilot study. *Journal of the Royal College of General Practitioners*, 38, pp 303-6.

Margolis, B.L., Kroes, W.H. and Quinn, R.P. (1974), Job stress: an Unlisted Occupational Hazard. *Journal of Occupational Medicine*, 16 (1-0), pp 654-61.

Marks, S.R. (1977), Multiple roles and role strain, *American Sociological Review*, 39, pp 567-578.

Marmot, M. and Brunner, E. (1991) Alcohol and cardiovascular disease: the status of the U-shaped curve. *British Medical Journal,*, 303, pp 365-8.

Maslach, C. and Jackson, S. (1986), *Maslach Burnout Inventory*. Consulting Psychologist's Press : Palo Alto: CA.

Matteson, M.T. and Ivancevich, J.M. (1987), Individual stress management interventions: Evaluation of techniques. *Journal of Managerial Psychology*, 2 (1), pp 24-30.

Mawardi, B.H. (1979), Satisfaction, dissatisfactions, and causes of stress in medical practice. *Journal of the American Medical Association*, 241, pp 1483-6.

McCrae, R.R., Costa, P.T. and Bosse, I.L. (1978), Anxiety, extroversion and smoking. *British Journal of Social and Clinical Psychology*, 17, pp 269-73.

McKenna, E. (1987), *Business Psychology and Organisational Behaviour*, Lawrence Erlbaum Associates Ltd: East Sussex, UK.

Mechanic, D. (1972), General medical practice: Some comparisons between the work of primary care physicians in the United States and England and Wales. *Public Expectations and Health Care*. Wiley: New York.

Medalie, J.H., Snyder, M., Groen, J.J., Nenfeld, N.H., Goldbourt, U. and Riss, E. (1973), Angina pectoris among 10,000 men, 5 year incidence and univariate analysis. *American Journal of Medicine*, 55, pp 583-94.

Medical Workforce Standing Advisory Committee: third report (1997), Planning the Medical Workforce, Department of Health, December.

Meichenbaum, D. (1979), *Cognitive-Behaviour Modification*. Plenum: New York.

Meichenbaum, D. (1985), *Stress Inoculation Training*. Pergamon: New York.

Meichenbaum, D. and Cameron, R. (1983), Stress inoculation training: Toward a general paradigm for training coping skills. In D. Meichenbaum and M.E. Jaremco (eds), *Stress Reduction and Prevention*, Plenum: New York.

Meichenbaum, D. and Turk, D. (1982), Stress, coping and disease: A cognitive-behavioural perspective. In R.W.J. Neufield (eds.), *Psychological Stress and Psychopathology*, McGraw-Hill: New York..

Melville, A. (1980), Job satisfaction in general practice: implications in prescribing. *Social Science and Medicine*, 14A, pp 495-9.

Miles, H.H., Waldfogel, S., Barrabee, E.L. and Cobb, S. (1954), Psychosomatic study of 46 young men with coronary artery disease. *Psychosomatic Medicine*, 16, p 955.

Miles, J.E., Krell, R. and Lin, R.Y. (1975), The doctors wife: mental illness and marital pattern. *International Journal of Psychiatry in Medicine*, 6, pp 481-7.

Modgil, S. (1986), 'Multilcultural Education, the Interminable debate'. In B.Wade and P.Souter (eds), *'Continuing to think: The British Asian girl. An exploratory study of the influence of culture upon a group of British Asian girls with specific reference to the teaching of English'*, Multilingual Matters: Cleavdon.

Modlin, H.C. and Monte, A. (1964), Narcotic addiction in physicians. *American Journal of Psychiatry*, 121, pp 358-65.

Monat, A. and Lazarus, R.S. (1991), *Stress and Coping - an Anthology*. 3rd Edition, Columbia University Press: New York.

Morrell, D.C., Evans, M.E., Morris, R.W., and Roland, M.O. (1986), The five minute consultation; effect of time constraint on clinical context and patient satisfaction. *British Medical Journal*, 292, pp 870-3.

Morris, J.N., Heady, J.A. and Barley, R.G. (1952), Coronary heart disease in medical practitioners. *British Medical Journal*, 1, pp 503-20.

Murray, R. (1983), The sick doctor. *Medicine Interne* 1(34), pp 1582-4

Murray, R.M. (1977), Psychiatric illness in male doctors and controls: an analysis of Scottish in-patient hospital data. *British Journal of Psychiatry*, 131, pp 1-10.

Murray, R.M. (1978), The health of doctors: a review. *Journal of the Royal College of Physicians*, 12 (5), pp 403-15.

Murray, R.M. (1983), The mentally ill doctor: causes and consequences. *Practitioner*, 222, pp 65-75.

Murray, R.M. (1976), Alcoholism amongst male doctors in Scotland. *Lancet; ii* : 729-33.

Myers, M.F. (1984), 'Treating Troubled Marriages'. *American Family Physician*, 29 January: pp 221-226.

Myers, M.F. (1994), *Doctors' Marriages: a Look at the Problems and Solutions*. Second Edition, Plenum Publishing Corporation: New York.

Myerson, S. (1990), Under Stress? *Practitioner*, 234, pp 973-6.

Nadelson, C., Notman, M. and Lowenstein, P. (1979), The practice pattern, life styles and stresses of women and men entering medicine: a follow-up study of Harvard Medical School graduates from 1967 to 1977. *Journal of the American Medical Women's Association*, 34, pp 400-6.

Nadelson, C. and Notman, M.T. (1983),. What is different for women physicians? In Scheiber, S.C., Doyle, B.E., (eds.) *The Impaired Physician*. Plenum: New York.

Nadelson, C. and Notman, M. (1979), Adaption to stress in physicians. In E. Shapiro and L. Lowensrein (eds.), *Becoming a physician*, Ballinger Publishing Company: Cambridge.

Nelson, S. (1978), Some dynamics of medical marriages. *Journal of the Royal College of General Practitioners*, 28, pp 585-7.

Norwood-East, W. (1949), British Journal of Addiction.;46:38. Cited in Murray L. *Journal of the Royal College of Physicians*, 1978;12(5), p 415.

Paget, M.D., Erdley, W.W. and Becker J. (1987), Social networks: we get by with (and in spite of), a little help from friends. *Journal of Personality and Social Psychology*, 53, pp 793-804.

Parkhouse, J. and Ellin, D.J. (1988), Reasons for doctors career choice and change of choice. *British Medical Journal*, 296, pp 1651-3.

Patel, C. (1973), Yoga and biofeedback in the management of hypertension. *Lancet. 2*, pp 1053-5.

Patel, C. and Marmot M.G. (1988), Can general practitioners use training in relaxation and management of stress to reduce mild hypertension? *British Medical Journal*, 296, pp 21-4.

Patel, C. and Marmot, M.G. (1987), Stress management, blood pressure and quality of life. *Journal of Hypertension 5: Supplement* 1, pp 21-6.

Patel, C. and North W.R.S. (1975), Randomised controlled trial of Yoga and biofeedback in the management of hypertension. *Lancet, 2*, pp 93-5.

Patel, C. Marmot M.G., Terry D.J., Carruthers, M., Hunt, B. and Patel, M. (1985), Trial of relaxation in reducing coronary risk: four year follow up. *British Medical Journal*, 290, 1103-6.

Pescor, M. (1942), Diseases of the Nervous System. 3:173. Cited in Murray R. *Journal of the Royal College of Physicians*. 1978;12, p 415.

Peterson, W.P. (1979), *Meditation made easy*. Franklin Watts: New York.

Peveler, R.C. and Johnston, D.W. (1986), Sublective and cognitive effects of relaxation. *Behaviour Research and Therapy*, 24, pp 413-9.

Plantenga, J (1995), Labour-Market Participation of Women in

European Union. In A. van Doorne-Huiskes, J. van Hoot and E. Ruelofs (eds), *Women and the European Labour Markets*, Paul Chapman: London. pp 1-14.

Pleck, J.H. (1985), *Working Wives/Working Husbands*, Sage: Beverly Hills, CA.

Pinder, R. (1997), "*Female GPs suffer time anxiety*". *GP* February 14, p 48.

Porter, A.M.D, Howie, J.G.R. and Levinson, A. (1985), Measurement of stress as it affects the work of the general practitioner. *Family Practice*, 2, pp 136-46.

Priestley, M.(1995), Commonality and difference in the movement: An "Association of Blind Asians" in Leeds. *Disability and Society*, 10 (June), pp 157-69.

Pullinger, J. (Ed.), (1998), Regenal Trends No. 33, The Stationery Office: London.

Putnam, P.L. and Ellingwood, E.H. Jr. (1966), Narcotic addiction among physicians: a ten year follow-up. *American Journal of Psychiatry*, 122, pp 745-8.

Quick, J.C., and Quick, J.D. (1984), *Organizational Stress and Preventive Management*. Mcgraw-Hill: New York.

Rahe, R., O'Neill, T.O. Hagan, A. and Arthur R.J. (1975), Brief group therapy following myocardial infarction- eighteen month follow-up of a controlled trial. *International Journal of Psychiatry in Medicine*, 6, pp 349-58.

Ramirez, A.J., Graham, J. Richards, M.A.. Cull, A., Gregory, W.M., Learing, M.S., Snashaft, D.C. and Timothy, A.R. (1995), Burnout and psychiatric disorder among cancer clinicians. *British Journal of Cancer*, 71, (6), pp 1263-9.

Rawnsley, K. (1989), Physician, don't heal thyself: let someone else try!. *Practitioner*, 233, pp 891.

Rawnsley, K. (1985), Helping the sick doctor: a new service. *British Medical Journal*, pp 291-923.

Rice, P.L. (1992), *Stress and Health, 2nd edition*, Book/Cole Publishing Company: California.

Richards, C. (1989), *The health of doctors*. King's Fund: London.

Richardson, A. and Burke, R. (1991), Occupational stress and job satisfaction and burnout among physicians: Sex differences.

Social Science and Medicine, 13, pp 1179-87.

Richardson, A.M. and Burke, R.J. (1993), Occupational stress and work satisfaction among Canadian physicians. *Psychological Report*, 72 , pp 711-821.

Richings, J.C., Khara, G.S. and McDowell, M. (1986), Suicide in young doctors. *British Journal of Psychiatry*, 149, pp 475-8.

Rimm, D.C. and Masters, J. C. (1979), *Behaviour Therapy: Techniques and empirical findings* (2nd eds), McGraw-Hill: New York.

Robinowitz, C.B. (1983.),The physician as a patient. In Scheiber S.C., Doyle B.B. (eds). *The Impaired Physician*. New York: Plenum.

Roeske, N.C.A. (1981), Stress and the physician. *Psychiatry Annals* 11, pp 245-58.

Rosa, K. (1976), *Autogenic Training*. Victor Gollancz: London.

Rosch, P.J. and Pelletier, K.R. (1987), Designing worksite stress management programme. In L.R. Murphy and T.F. Schoenborn (eds). *Stress Management in Work Settings:* NIOSH.

Rose, K.D. and Rosow I. (1973), Physicians who kill themselves. *Archives of General Psychiatry*, 29, pp 800-5.

Rosenman, R.H. (1978), The interview model of assessment of the coronary-prone behaviour pattern. In Dembroski, T.M., Weiss, S.M., Sields, I.L., Haynes, S.G. and Feinlieb, M. (eds). *Coronary-Prone Behaviour*. New York: Springer-Verlag. pp 55-69.

Rosenman, R.H., Friedman, M. and Strauss, R. (1966), C.H.D. in the Western Collaborative Group Study. *Journal of the American Medical Association*. 195, pp 86-92.

Rout, U.and Rout, J.K. (1993), *Stress and General Practitioners*. Kluwer Academic Publishers: London.

Rout, U. and Rout, J.K (1997), Mental health, job stress and satisfaction among practice nurses: a pilot study, in M. K. Ross and C. Stark (eds), *Promoting Mental Health*, Ross and Stark: Scotland, pp 417–23.

Rout, U. (1986), *Occupational stress in general practitioners* MSc Dissertation, UMIST.

Rout, U. (1989), *Occupational stress in general practitioners* PhD Thesis, UMIST.

Rout, U. (1995), Occupational stress among general practitioners; In D.R. Trent and C.A. Reed (eds), *Promotion of Mental Health*, Vol. 5. Ashgate Publishing Ltd: Aldershot, pp 29-39.

Rout, U. (1996), Stress among general practitioners and their spouses: a qualitative study, *British Journal of General Practice*, 46, pp 157-60.

Rout, U. (1999), Gender differences in stress, satisfaction and mental well-being among general practitioners in England. *Psychology, Health and Medicine*, 4 (4), pp 345-54.

Rout, U. (1999), Occupational stress in women general practitioners and practice managers. *Women in Management Review*. 14(6), pp 220-29.

Rout, U. (1999), Stress and job satisfaction among primary care professionals, *Journal of International Professional Care*, 13 (4), pp 426-427.

Rout, U. (2000), Stress and health in health professionals, International conference on clinical psychology proceedings, Murcia, Spain (In press).

Rout, U. (1999), Job stress among general practitioners and nurses in primary care in England. *Psychological Reports*; 85: pp 981-86.

Rout, U. and Rout J. (1999), Identifying job stress among hospital consultants in England: an exploratory study, European Congress on Work and Organisational Psychology Conference: Helsinki.

Rout, U. and Rout, J.(1998), *Job stress and satisfaction amongst hospital consultants: an exploratory study*, Second World Congress on Stress: Melbourne, Australia.

Rout, U. and Rout, J.K. (1994), Job satisfaction, mental health and job stress among general practitioners before and after the new contract-a comparative study. *Family Practice*, 1, pp 300-6.

Rout, U. and Rout, J. (1996), Diagnosis and treatment of depression by general practitioners in England, *Psychological Reports*, 78: pp 516-18.

Rout, U. and Rout, J.K. (1997), A comparative study on occupational stress, job satisfaction and mental health in British general practitioners and Canadian family physicians. *Psychology, Health and Medicine*, 2 (2), pp 181-90.

Rout, U., Cooper, C.L. and Kerslake, H. (1997), Working and non-working mothers: a comparative study. *Women in Management Review*, 12 (7,8), pp 264-75.

Rout, U., Cooper, C.L. and Rout, J.K. (1996), Job stress among British general practitioners: predictors of job satisfaction and mental ill-health. *Stress Medicine*, 12, pp 155-66.

Rout, U. Sixsmith, J. and Moore, M. (1996), Asian family life. In More, Sixsmith and Knowle (Eds) *Children's reflections on family life*, Falmers Press. London. pp 100-14.

Rucinski, T. and Lybulsha, E. (1985), Mentally ill doctors. *British Journal of Hospital Medicine*, February, pp 90-4.

Russek, H.I. and Sohan B.L. (1960), Relative significance of hereditary, diet and occupational stress in CHD of young adults. *American Journal of Medical Sciences*, 235, pp 266-75.

Russek H.I (1959), Role of hereditary, diet and emotional stress in coronary heart disease. *Journal of the American Medical Association*, 171, pp 503-8.

Rutherford, R.D. (1978), Administrative time power: Meeting the time challenge of the busy secretary/staff assistant/manager/team. *Learning Concepts*: Austin, Texas.

Sakinofsky, I. (1980), Suicide in doctors and their wives. *British Medical Journal*, 281, pp 386-7.

Salmons, P.H. (1983), Psychiatric illness in medical students. *British Journal of Psychiatry*, 143, pp 505-8.

Sandlin, N. (1990), Physicians wed thyself, *American Medical News*, January 19, pp 29-32.

Sargent, D.A. (1986), *Physician suicide*. A paper presented at the annual meeting of the American College of Psychiatrists: Marco Island

Scheiber, S.C. (1977), Emotional problems of physicians: I. Nature and extent of problems. *Arizona Medicine*, 34, pp 323-5.

Scheiber, S.C. (1987), Stress in physicians. In. R. Payne and Firth-Cozens (eds), *Stress in the health professions*, Wiley: New York, pp 23-44.

Schuckit, M.A. and Gunderson, E.K.E. (1973), Job stress and psychiatric illness in the US Navy. *Journal of Occupational Medicine*, 15, pp 884-7.

Schultz, J. and Luthe, W. (1959), *Autogenic Training. A*

Psychophysiologic Approach to Psychotherapy, Grune and Stratton: New York.

Schultz, J. and Luthe, W. (1969), *Autogenic therapy. Autogenic methods*. Grune and Stratton: New York.

Schwartz, A.H., Schwartzburg, M., Lieb, J. and Slaby, A.E. (1978), Medical school and the process of disillusionment. *Medical Education*, 12 , pp 182-5.

Sekaran U. (1983), Factors affecting the quality of life in dual career families. *Journal of Occupational Psychology*, 56, pp 161-74.

Shekelle, R.B., Gayle, M., Ostfeld, A. and Paul, O. (1983), Hostility, risk of coronary heart disease, and mortality. *Psychosomatic Medicine*, 45, pp 109-14.

Simpson, J.A. and Grant, L. (1991), Source and magnitude of job stress among physicians. *Journal of Behavioural Medicine*, 14, (1), pp 27-42.

Social Trends (1983), London: HMSO.

Social Trends (1994), London: HMSO.

Spielburger, C.D. Johnson, E.H. Russell, S.F. (1985), The experience and expression of anger: construction and validation of an anger expression scale. In M.A. Chesney and R.H. Rosenman (eds), *Anger and hostility in cardio vascular and behavioural disorders*, Hemisphere/Magro-Hill: New York.

Stampfer, M.J. Colditz, G.A. Willett, W.C. et al (1988). A prospective study of moderate alcohol consumption and the risk of coronary disease in women. *New England Journal of Medicine*, 319, pp 267-73.

Stephens, M.A.P., Kinney, J.M. Norris, V.K. and Ritchie, S.W. (1987), Social networks as assets and liabilities in recovery from stroke by geriatric patients. *Psychology of Ageing*, 2, pp 141-52.

Steppacher, R.C. and Mausner, J.S. (1974), Suicide in male and female physicians. *Journal of the American Medical Association*, 228, pp 323-8.

Stewart, S.M., Betson, C., Marshall, I., Wong, C.M., Lee, P.W. and Lam, T.H. (1995*)*, Stress and vulnurability in medical students. *Medical Education,*; 29 (2), pp 119-27.

Stopes-Row, M., and Cochrane, R. (1990), The child-rearing values of Asian and British parents and young people: an inter-ethnic and inter-generational comparison in the evaluation of Kohn's 13 qualities. *British Journal of Social Psychology*, 29, pp 149-60.

Suinn, R.M. (1976), How to break the vicious cycle of stress. *Psychology Today*, 10, pp 59-60.

Suls, J. (1982), Social support, international relations and health: Benefits and liabilities. In G. S. Sanders and J. Suls (eds), *Social psychology of health and illness*. Erlbaum: Hillsdale, NJ.

Sutherland,V. and Cooper, C.L. (1990), *Understanding stress*, Chapman and Hall: London.

Sutherland,V. and Cooper, C.L. (1996), Stress in the offshore oil and gas exploration and production industries: An organizational approach to stress control. *Stress Medicine*, 12, pp 27-34.

Sutherland, V. and Cooper, C.L. (1987), *Man and Accidents Offshore*. Lloyds: London.

Sutherland,V.J. and Davidson, M.J. (1989), Stress among Construction site Managers. A preliminary Study. *Stress Medicine*, pp 221-35.

Sutherland, V.J., and Cooper, C.L. (1992), Job stress, satisfaction and mental health among GPs before and after the introduction of the New Contract. *British Medical Journal*, 304, pp 1545-8.

Swanson, V. Power, K and Simpson, R. (1996), A comparison of stress and job satisfaction in female and male general practitioners and consultants, *Stress Medicine*, 12, pp 17-26.

Swanson, V., Power, K. and Simpson, R. (1998), Occupational Stress and family life: A comparison of male and female doctors, *Journal of Occupational and Organisational Psychology*, 71 (3), pp 237-60.

Symons, L. and Persaud, R. (1995), Stress among doctors. *British Medical Journal*, 310 (6981), p 742.

Talbot, G.D., Gallegos, K.V., Wilson, P.O. and Porter, T.L. (1987), The medical association of Georgia's impaired physician programme. Review of first 1000 physicians : Analysis of speciality. *Journal of the American Medical Association*, 257 (21), pp 227-30.

Taylor, N.D., Sinclair, A. and Wall, A.M. (1987*)*, Sources of stress in postgraduate medical training. *Journal of Medical Education*, 62 pp 425-8.

The Impaired Physician. AMA. Department of Mental Health. Conference on the impaired physicians, September, 1978.

Theorell, T. (1977), Selected illness and somatic factors in relation to two psychosocial stress indices - a prospective study on middle aged construction building workers. *Journal of Psychosomatic Research*, 20, pp 7-20.

Theorell, T. and Karasek, R.A. (1996) Current issues relating to psychosocial job strain and cardiovascular disease research. *Journal of Occupational Health Psychology*, 1, pp 9-26.

Thoits, P. (1983), Multiple identities and psychological well-being. *American Sociological Review*, 48, pp 174-187.

Turner, J., Tippett, V. and Raphael, H. (1994), Women in medicine – socialization, stereotypes and self perceptions. *Australian and New Zealand Journal of Psychiatry*, 28 (1), pp 129-135.

Uhlenberg, P. and Cooney, T. (1990), Male and Female Physicians: family and career comparisons, *Social Science and Medicine*, 30, pp 373-8.

Ulett, G.A. and Paterson, D.B. (1965), *Applied Hypnosis and positive suggestion*. C.V. Mosby: St. Louis.

Vaillant, G.E., Sobowale N.C. and McArthur C. (1972), Some psychologic vulnerabilities of physicians. *New England Journal of Medicine*, 287, pp 372-5.

Vaillant, G.E., Brighton, J.R. and McArthur, C. (1970), Physicians' use of mood-altering drugs : A 20 year follow-up report. *New England Journal of Medicine*, 282, pp 365-72.

Valko, U. and Clayton, P.L. (1975) Depression in the internship. *Diseases of the Nervous System*, 36, pp 26-9.

Van Sell, M., Brief, A.P. and Schuler, R.S. (1981), Role conflict and role ambiguity: Integration of the literature and directions for future research. *Human Relations*, 34 (1), pp 43-71.

Vaux, A. (1988), *Social Support: Theory, Research, and Intervention*. Praeger: New York.

Verbrugge, L.M. (1982), Women's social roles and health. In P. Berman and E. Ramey (eds), *Women: A Developmental Perspective*. National Institute of Health: Bethesda, MD, pp. 49-78.

Vernon, S.W., Roberts, R.E. and Lee, E.S. (1984), Ethnic status and participation in longitudinal health studies. *American Journal of*

Epidemiology, 119, pp 99-113.
Wall, J.H. (1958), Federation Bulletin. 45:144. Cited in Murray R. *Journal of the Royal College of Physicians,* 1978; 12(5), pp 415.
Waring, E.M. (1974), Emotional illness in psychiatric trainees. *British Journal of Psychiatry.* 125, pp 10-11.
Weisman, C.S. and Teitelbaum, M.A. (1987), The work-family role system and physician productivity. *Journal of Health and Social Behaviour.* 28, pp 247-57.
Weiss, J.M. (1984) Behavioural and psychological influences on gastrointestinal pathology: experimental techniques and findings. In W.D. Gentry (eds), *Hand book of Behavioural Medicine*: New York: Guilford.
Werner, E.R., Adler, R., Robinson, R. and Korsch, B.M. (1979), Attitudes and interpersonal skills during paediatric internship. *Paediatrics.* 63(3), pp 491-9.
Westwood, S. and Bhachu, P. (1987); *Enterprising Women, Ethnicity, Economy and Gender Relations.* Routledge: London.
White, D. and Woollett, A (1992), *'Families, a context for development',* The Falmer Press: London.
Wilhelmsen, L. (1980), Stress and coronary heart disease. *Australian and New Zealand Journal of Medicine,* 10, pp 135-8.
Williams, S.V., Munford, R.S., Colton, T., Murphy, D.A. and Poskanzer, D.C. (1971), Mortality among physicians: a cohort study. *Journal of Chronic Diseases.* 24, pp 393-401.
Williams, A.P., Pierre, A.D. and Vayda, E. (1993), Women in medicine: Towards a conceptual understanding of the potential for change. *Journal of American Medical Women's Association.* 48 (4), pp 115-21.
Williams, S. Dale, J. Glucksman, E. and Wellesley, A. (1997),. Senior house officers' work related stressors, psychological distress, and confidence in performing clinical tasks in accident and emergency: a questionnaire study. *British Medical Journal,* 314, pp 713-8.
Wittkower, E.D. and Warnes, H., (eds), (1977), *Psychosomatic Medicine: Its clinical Applications,* Harper and Row: New York.
Wolf, T.M. (1994), Stress, coping and health: enhancing well-being during medical school. *Medical Education,* 28 (1), pp 55-7.

Wolf, T.M. and Kissling, G.E. (1984), Changes in lifestyle characteristics, health, and mood of freshman medical students. *Journal of Medical Education.* 59, pp 806-14.

Wolf, T.M., Balson, P.M., Faucett, J.M. and Randall, H.M. (1989), A retrospective study of attitude change during medical education. *Journal of Medical Education.* 23, pp 19-23.

Wolpe, J. (1973), *The Practice of Behaviour Therapy.* Pergamon: New York.

Wolpe, J. (1958), *Psychotherapy by Reciprocal Inhibition.* Stanford University Press.

Young, G. and Spencer, J. (1996), General practitioners' views about the need for a stress support service. *Family Practice,* 13 (6), pp 517-21.

Ziegler, P.P. (1992), Dealing with Stress in the Physician's Marriage. *Pennsylvania Medicine.* (June), pp 38-41.

Ziegler. P.P. (1991), Coping with stress in physician's family. *Physician's Practice Digest,* 2, pp 53-6.